Quit Hiding, Start Living!

How Women Can Free Themselves From Past Hurts

To MONICA
Arise and shine for your
light hey come and The glory
of The Lord is risen upon you.
November 2016

by

GLADYS FAMORIYO

First published in Great Britain in 2012
By GF Books Ltd – Changing lives through words
Tel: +44 (0)870 750 1969
www.gladysfbooks.com

1 3 5 7 9 10 8 6 4 2

Printed and bound in Great Britain by
Berforts Information Press Ltd.

Book cover design: Tash Mountford
Typeset in Sabon 10pt by www.chandlerbookdesign.co.uk

ISBN 978-0-9562606-6-6

Praise for Quit Hiding, Start Living! by Gladys Famoriyo

"*Quit Hiding, Start Living* is an insightful read which peers into the recesses of the heart and asks some deep and searching questions about where we find ourselves and how we got there. Engaging in the 'Journaling' segments gives the reader a chance to answer those questions in an open and truthful manner with the comfort of the 'Enlightening Moments' bringing insight and guidance.

If you find yourself identifying with the 'hiding woman' syndrome, this book is both therapeutic and inspirational as it encourages healing and the vision to move forward to a more fulfilling life.

Gladys' book, *Quit Hiding, Start Living! How Women Can Free Themselves From Past Hurts* is an excellent volume which I will certainly use alongside my work with 'hurting' women. I run a course titled *Forgiveness as Healing* which deals with how to forgive in a way that will help you heal from past hurts. *Quit Hiding, Start Living!* will encourage positive introspective thinking which is necessary for someone struggling with forgiveness and the inability to overcome hurts. Want a prescription for healing? Read the book and embrace a more abundant life."

- **Sharon Platt-McDonald** (Director of Health, Disability & Women Ministries, British Union Conference of The Seventh-day Adventist UK). Author, *Healing Hearts; Restoring Minds* and *Extending The Olive Branch: Forgiveness As Healing*

* * *

"How many women have been hurt, betrayed and abused? The figure is higher than we might care to think about. How many are too ashamed to admit and talk about what has happened? All too often, such women hide their shame, grief and anger inside and try to carry on as usual. All too often the repressed emotional anguish can come out in physical pain and disturbances in bodily function and treated by drugs with limited success. The fact that unexplained illnesses like Irritable Bowel Syndrome are so much commoner in women than men may represent this hidden hurt.

In her latest book, *Quit Hiding, Start Living! How Women Can Free Themselves From Past Hurts*, Gladys Famoriyo encourages women to open up their hearts, acknowledge what has happened and start living.

A dedicated teacher, the compassion and understanding expressed in her book will be an inspiration for the multitude of women nursing unresolved hurt and shame, often in physical illness."

- **Professor Nick Read** (Physician and Psychotherapist. Director of The IBS Network, the national charity for patients with Irritable Bowel Syndrome www.theibsnetwork.org) Author, *Sick And Tired, Healing The Illnesses Doctors Cannot Cure.*

Quit Hiding, Start Living!

by

GLADYS FAMORIYO

C O N T E N T S

Dedication   xi

Acknowledgements   xiii

Preface   xv

How to get the best out of this book   xix

A story   xxi

Part 1
Discovering the trapped princess in you   1

1. When we lock ourselves away   3
    Hiding as a means of escape   4
    Struggling to cope behind closed doors   7
    Old issues, modern castles   10

2. A tale of two princesses   15
    The beautiful flower that closed up for good 15
    Me, God and no one else!   20

3. Discovering the trapped princess in you   29
    Common traits of hurting, trapped princesses 30
    Understanding how your body responds   43

4. Pulling away from the crowds   53
    God's perspective on retreating   56
    When retreats go wrong   57

Part 2
Letting the drawbridge down   **63**

5.	Experiencing freedom from hurt	65
	Breaking free from your castle	68
	Giving God access to your heart	72

6.	Starting your personal journey	79
	Preparing for your retreat	81
	Embarking upon your retreat	85

7.	Uncover your hurtful experiences	89
	Getting clearer	90
	Recognising patterns and themes	101
	Giving your cares to God	104

8.	Forgive, and love again	109
	A lesson on love	109
	From love to forgiveness	111
	A case for forgiving	113
	Now, over to you	115

9.	Unlock your heart and install gates!	123
	Allowing people access to your heart	123
	Guarding your heart	133
	Put boundaries in place	137

10.	Build healthy relationships	143
	You won't get on with everyone!	146
	Not everyone will be your friend	148
	Forging healthy relationships	149

11.	Quit hiding – for good!	155
	Choose to stay out of the castle	155
	Deal with 'people' issues as they arise	156

Closing thoughts   159

    Remember who you are   159
    Consider the bigger picture   161

Epilogue

Princess Leanne revisited   165

About the author   167

Also available from the author   **171**

Also available from GF Books LTD   **179**

Initiatives from the author –   185
The Gladys Famoriyo Academy

Initiatives from the author –
The Overcoming Emotional Baggage Women's   187
Conference & Initiative

Initiatives from the author – eWoman Groups   189

My Notes   193

Dedication

To all the women and young girls of the world who have been wounded, abused, raped, rejected, overlooked, excluded, heartbroken, wronged or betrayed; or have been made to feel ashamed, guilty, afraid or worthless ... I dedicate this book to you.

Whoever you are and wherever you find yourself today, may you find peace, comfort and healing as you read this book.

Acknowledgements

s usual, I would like to thank my Heavenly Father for His constant love, grace and compassion towards me. You are my ever-faithful, ever-present, ever-constant Companion. Because of Your steadfast love, I can confidently face my tomorrows with an inexplicable peace. My heart is overwhelmed daily by the fact that I am constantly on Your mind. That, in itself, blows my mind!

I would like to take this opportunity to thank all those who have supported me on my fourth writing project.

Mother dearest (Pastor Joyce Famoriyo), thanks for being my greatest encourager, incessant intercessor, dearest friend and ardent supporter. You have stood by me through thick and thin. For such, I will always remain grateful to you and God (who divinely connected us for such a time as this).

To my dear family, friends and mentors – thank you for your love and support through the years. To my 'book writing' team – thank you for making the vision a reality.

Preface

When you have been hurt by life, love, and others, how do you react?

Perhaps you say, 'I just move on.'

This is a great attitude to adopt, but the harsh reality for many of us – young and old – is that we find moving on often difficult to achieve. Many of us get stuck and, as a result of our hurtful life experiences, we resort to hiding, not knowing what else to do. On the surface we may look OK – we learn to wear a mask. But, underneath, you will discover a heart scored with deep, oozing wounds.

And so, hiding becomes the strategy we adopt. It is a form of self-preservation but, while it can help in the short term (getting away to a 'quiet' place where we can process the hurt before moving on), if we stay hiding it will end up having a detrimental effect on us. In a bid to stop the 'hurter' or potential 'hurters' wounding us, we construct barriers around ourselves. Then, when we look at life through the tinted lenses of our hurts, trusting people – and even God – becomes a real issue, even when they pose no threat to us. We bolt up the doors to our hearts and put up a sign that says: 'Love don't live here anymore' – or simply: 'No entry'.

You too may have found yourself withdrawing from others, even unconsciously. It does not have to be a physical withdrawing – it can also be spiritual and/or emotional. It is not that you have fled to a secluded island: you still live in society but, while you are here in body, your heart is disengaged. Not only do you do your utmost to avoid any situations where you might get hurt, but also you no longer connect emotionally with others or make yourself vulnerable in any way.

So it is that, over time, you might find yourself cut off from others. You know you need to open the doors of your heart but it has been locked up for so long. You have lost the keys and cannot get out. Your hiding antics have trapped you – no one can get in … but you find that you are unable to leave.

If you recognize that hiding may have been your way dealing with your hurtful life experiences, this book has been written with you in mind. And what we both know (or you would not be reading this book) is that remaining this way is not healthy. It is certainly not God's best for any of His daughters (or sons, for that matter).

I intend to share with you some insights I have picked up along the way after being hurt myself. My desire is to support you in moving past your hurts, unlocking your heart and learning to (re)connect with people again. You will learn how to get rid of your hiding tendencies, while also knowing how to withdraw from the crowds in a healthy way when necessary. (I call this retreating.) Safeguarding your heart is still a necessary and wise thing to do, and I will share with you how you can let down the drawbridge to your heart – whilst installing simple gates for a little self-protection.

How to get the best out of this book

This book is all about putting into practice everything you learn. I have constructed it in such a way that working through its pages should be a natural progression for you. The first part of the book describes the place many of us find ourselves in today. I do this by sharing stories of trapped women (including my former self) and their traits – and how their stories relate to us. I also prepare you for your own journey by sharing insights about how to withdraw effectively – a positive 'retreat' – which can be a powerful tool.

In the latter part of the book you will find the practical part. Here I share key points which will set you on your journey – a journey where you will experience freedom from the entanglements of your hurts, build healthy relationships, and stay out of hiding. To help you break down the walls that you have built between yourself and others, I have included some reflective questions in the 'Journaling Moments'; food for thought in the 'Enlightening Moments'; and inspiring biblical quotes.

All I ask of you is to keep an open mind and prepare it to receive all that is in store for you. I pray that this book reaches those parts of you that have been locked away. I hope and pray it penetrates deep into your heart and soul, where its lessons can take root and blossom bountifully in your life and that of others.

Enjoy the journey!

A story

The trapped princess

Once upon a time there was a beautiful princess whose name was Leanne. Princess Leanne lived in a large, pretty castle which was surrounded by a deep moat filled with water. The castle sat on the edge of a deep forest and the only way to get into it was across the drawbridge – one which only the princess could open.

Each morning, Princess Leanne would get up and dress herself in the most beautiful dresses and shoes which her father, the king, had given to her before he travelled to a faraway land. As well as many other precious gifts, including a diamond-encrusted jewellery box, he gave his daughter the keys to the drawbridge before he left, so that she could go out whenever she wanted or invite her friends over.

Each day, Princess Leanne longed for her father to return home. Although she lived in such a beautiful castle, she was always sad and lonely. At first, she did not want to admit this to herself and she kept herself busy reading books, drawing, or playing music. And, although those things were fun to begin with, as the years went by she became more sad and lonely. No one ever came to visit her nor did she go out.

Life never used to be like this for Princess Leanne. When she was a child, her father always took her on outings. They would visit the forest, play hide and seek, and have picnics by the river. He even taught her how to catch fish. They had so much fun. He encouraged her to have tea parties and balls in the castle and invite all her friends, as well as other princes and princesses from kingdoms far and near. But none of this had happened since her father had left.

Before the king took his leave he reminded Leanne of her duties. She was to leave the castle every day and visit parts of their great kingdom in turn – as was expected of a princess while her father was absent. Part of her royal duties included visiting the subjects of the kingdom and inviting them to the castle, as well as organising events such as the children's Easter fête, the summer barbeque, and the harvest celebration for everyone in the kingdom.

At first, Princess Leanne was afraid of going out by herself but then she remembered her father's words about her responsibilities and soon got over her fear. She would take long walks in the forest or, sometimes, meet her friends for picnics down by the river. She would visit the subjects of the kingdom – both far and near. They grew to love her and always gave her a warm welcome.

Princess Leanne thoroughly enjoyed her days out as well as having guests to the castle. Then, one day, as she was returning to the castle after a long walk, a huge, wicked dragon came out of nowhere. He wanted to capture her and take her away to his evil kingdom far, far away. There he planned to keep her prisoner, locked up in his dungeon. Leanne knew that if the dragon caught her she would never see her beloved father again, so she ran as fast as she could, falling down many times. Eventually, she made it to the castle and pulled up the drawbridge quickly. Then she locked it and hid away the key. From that day, Princess Leanne never set foot outside the castle. Nor did she lower the drawbridge to let anyone inside.

Day after day, her friends would ask her to come out and play but she was so terrified at the thought of coming across the wicked dragon again that she would not let the drawbridge down. And so, after a while, they stopped calling round. And, even though her subjects assured her that the wicked dragon had been chased away to a faraway land, she would not come out. She felt too scared and traumatized to do so.

So that is how Princess Leanne kept herself locked up for years, following her childhood encounter with the wicked dragon. She had promised herself she would never to go out again and she remained adamant. There were times when she considered leaving the castle, but then she remembered how terrified the wicked dragon had made her feel. So she dismissed the idea: 'Oh no! I dare not leave the safety of my castle. The dragon would only try to hurt me again.'

So there she remained – year in, year out. Leanne never attended any of the outings to which she was invited: those balls hosted by princesses and princes of other kingdoms, or even her friends' parties. Neither did she organise the annual kingdom events, even though the king and his subjects had expected it of her. As a result there were a great many people in the kingdom who were disgruntled, as they looked forward to them every year.

As the years went by, people ceased inviting Princess Leanne to any events – knowing that there was little point in doing so – and she missed her friends' weddings, birthdays and much more. And when handsome princes from faraway kingdoms wanted her hand in marriage, they left disappointed when she would not lower the drawbridge to her castle.

Each day, from her beautiful balcony, Princess Leanne would watch people of her kingdom pass by. She would see them having picnics in the forest, and the children playing. She could never understand why they never seemed afraid of the wicked dragon. Their fears never stopped them from enjoying the beauty of the forest – its huge trees, beautiful flowers, and friendly animals. They always seemed happy, unlike her.

Then, one day – many years later – Princess Leanne got so lonely that she decided it was time to step out of the castle. She gingerly headed towards the drawbridge to unlock it but could not find the keys. She searched everywhere – but it had been so long since she had used them that she could not remember where they were. Moreover, she had forgotten the secret code her father had given her in case she lost the keys.

With no keys or secret code, Princess Leanne was truly trapped inside her castle. It was then that she started to cry great floods of tears because she wanted to get out but did not know how. She wished her father would come home and help her and she sobbed, 'Father, where are you?'

*   *   *

When I first started writing this book, the image of a beautiful fairytale princess trapped in her gorgeous castle stuck in my mind. Then it occurred to me that I could use the story as an allegory in the book. I figured that many of us were living like Princess Leanne: after our hurtful 'wicked dragon' moments, we react just like her and hide ourselves in the castles of our hearts. Then we find that the very place we sought for safety and solace becomes our prison, trapping us.

This prison we create prevents us from enjoying healthy relationships. It is also the reason for the deep sense of sadness, pain and loneliness in our hearts. Some of us, when we decide to venture out eventually, find that we seem to have lost the keys. We no longer have the know-how to unlock the drawbridge to our heart so that we can build relationships. And so we remain trapped for years. Cut off from others, we feel exasperated, isolated, helpless and hopeless.

The good news is that we do not have to remain there. And this book explores how we can gain freedom from past hurts and live the life I believe God intended for us all.

Part 1

Discovering the trapped
princess in you

Chapter One

When we lock ourselves away

If you have ever been hurt, there is a chance you may have found yourself saying, 'I'm never going to let that happen to me again!' After that, you will go to great lengths to do whatever it takes to avoid any situation that vaguely resembles the situation that hurt you before. In Princess Leanne's case, her encounter with a wicked dragon traumatized her so badly that she locked herself away not only from the dragon, but also other people – and life – figuring this would protect her. And, as we know, her actions had the opposite effect, doing more harm than good.

That was how Princess Leanne handled her problems. Do we, as modern women, handle our traumatic 'wicked dragon' moments differently? The answer is no. Nothing has changed – we handle them in exactly the same way!

Lola

'I'm never going to let that happen to me again!' were the sentiments of Lola, the 45-year-old successful, self-made business mogul I mentioned in my previous book, *Healing A Discouraged Heart: Getting Back On Track When Life Lets You Down* (ISBN 978-0-9562606-3-5). After a string of failed relationships, including her most recent with Steve – her ex-fiancé – who broke her heart by breaking the relationship off without any explanation, she resigned never to delve into a romantic relationship again. After all, she had been hurt one too many times. Not wanting to experience the pain, rejection and heartache again, she was resigned to giving her entire focus to her businesses and charitable projects.

Hiding as a means of escape

Ok, so you don't live in a beautiful castle but you live somewhere or have some form of private space, right?

It could be a room in your parents'/guardian's home, a shared flat, bed-sit, university campus, your own home, office, or simply your half of a bed. Regardless of where it is, you have a safe place where you can run to when you feel hurt by people or life. It is the place over which you feel you have power. Here, you can determine who comes into your space. This is your safe haven where you feel you can shut out even the risk of harm.

Some people use writing in a notebook or a journal (which they might lock away) to escape their pain. In this way, their writing becomes a form a castle. And when feel we have no physical place to hide, we find we can use our minds, engaging them as a tool – giving us a virtual space into which we can retreat.

The problem arises when people retreat so deeply into their minds that it instigates a barrage of other issues, which ultimately affect their mental health.

Wherever we escape to or whatever method we adopt, the process is the same: behind the closed doors of our hearts we recount our ordeal. Time after time, the hurtful event continues to replay in our minds like a scratched record. There is nothing and no one to help us break the cycle or heal our wounded selves. Our mind cannot seem to stop reliving our 'wicked dragon' encounters. We are still hurting and as mad as hell. Our wounds are sore and badly in need of attention as was in the case of Krista.

Krista

'But I can't stop thinking about it!' Krista kept saying to me when she called my office to talk about her lifelong, painful challenges with men. She too had been heartbroken by a man who had been enthusiastic about her at the start but had become increasingly withdrawn. The fact that he kept blowing hot and cold meant Krista never quite knew where she stood with him. Her emotions having been toyed with in this way, she had become distraught. Day and night, the whole saga played over in her mind – so much so that she had lost weight and 'her pain' (as she put it) was now affecting the quality of her life. 'Why can't I get him out of my mind? I wish I could make it all go away,' she said.

Then, as if that was not enough, a barrage of emotional baggage shows up, and we experience the full weight of anger, bitterness, hatred, lack of forgiveness, guilt, and shame. In this state, you might think that it would make sense to call for help – but the idea is most often quickly dismissed. If we were to reach out for help it would mean: 1) we would have to open the door, and then the wicked dragon might gain access again; or 2) we might open up ourselves to new potential dragons. Like Princess Leanne and Lola, we deem asking for help to be too risky. So we opt to keep the door shut and we recoil further into our castles.

It is no surprise that, with the amount of time we spend behind the walls we erect between ourselves and the rest of humanity, we never get any closer to experiencing a healing of our wounds. Very little, if anything, has changed: the condition of our heart is very much the same. This should not be surprising to us – after all, we have set out without an agenda or support.

And even though we know hiding away will prove damaging for our emotional and physical health, for us modern princesses it remains the tool of choice.

Struggling to cope behind closed doors

You may be thinking, 'I have not locked myself away!'

This is probably true – at least not in any obviously physical way. I have yet to meet any princess who boarded a spaceship bound for Mars after her dude went off and married her best friend or as a result of a perturbing life situation. Many simply respond as Lola did. When we have been hurt by life, most of us do not get the chance to take time out – let alone relocate to another place (or planet) – so that we can try to make sense of what happened and move on.

When I am hurting, I always have a desire to get away from it all – even if it is only for a little while. (Perhaps it's the Princess Leanne in me.) On occasion, I have been known to ask God to kindly stop the world from rotating so that I can jump off and have a break – letting me back on when I am good and ready. He is yet to answer that prayer, by the way, but you had better watch out – just in case the world comes to a grinding halt all of a sudden!

Many of us find ourselves back on the treadmill of life, all too quickly – running at the same pace as before, that which is expected of us – whilst hurting, broken, bleeding, grieving, wounded, assailed, and traumatized. We continue to be the dutiful wife, doting mother, supportive friend, loving daughter, high-flying professional, business owner, achieving student, godly single woman, wise granny, and much more. We fix our faces so that we can face the world. That way, we can appear as if everything is fine in our world.

Deep inside, there may be a Princess Leanne locked away. In this state, we can never be our very best, though it never stops us from striving to be so. In my book *Overcoming Emotional Baggage: A Woman's Guide to Living the Abundant Life* (ISBN 0-924748-73-7), I describe our efforts as pouring water into a sieve and expecting it to get full. Why? Because although we strive to fill ourselves, every day we leak!

With our Princess Leanne selves neatly tucked away behind our latest fashionable outfits, our success, busyness, roles and responsibilities, we simply get out there and perform – something I am all too familiar with. We step into another persona when the curtains of life rise, and we perform. Our audience is waiting; we dare not let them down because they have paid a price to see us do our 'thing'. Then, once the curtains come down again, we retreat.

If you care to look back, you will remember that carrying all those burdens whilst trying to be the woman God called you to be, was hard work. But, whilst God is gracious in His mercies to carry us through such times, I do not believe that this is how He desires us to live our lives. We need Him every step of the way while we carry on with our everyday lives, striving to fulfil our purpose. But our hurts and emotional baggage can become the substance that clogs up our pipelines and hinders His Spirit to move freely through us.

I remember the time when my Dad passed away suddenly. There was a whole mixture of emotions flying about, in addition to the grief itself. I felt hurt and angry at God for taking my Dad away. And I was hurt and angry at my father for dying. I had a lack of forgiveness in my heart towards him and at the time I did not get the chance to resolve these, and other, issues. In a way, I felt cheated: I would never hear him say, 'Gladys, I'm sorry'. And, of course, there was the girl in me who suddenly realised I would never hear my daddy's voice again or see his smile. We would never again compare notes of the places we had travelled to, or make plans to visit new places. I would never see him do his funny 'dad' dances or hear him call me 'little' – his pet name for me.

I was not coping well with Dad's passing away (which opened up a whole can of worms), yet I carried on, business as usual. 'Whose funeral?' I kept wondering in shock and denial. Deep inside I wanted to flee from it all – and simply 'be' for a while – but we had a funeral to plan. Like David in Psalm 55: 6–7, I wished I had wings like a dove so I could fly away to a far quiet place and rest. If I could only get away, I thought to myself, I would be fine.

So many times, in the aftermath of my father's death, I wanted to bolt out of the door and just disappear. When the onslaught of people came round – day and night – I wanted to slink into my car and shut myself away from it all. But I didn't. Instead, I suffered in silence and, looking back, I wish I had carved out some time for myself and managed to fight off the idea that people might be thinking I was selfish. How I wished I knew what I know now! It would have shortened my grieving.

You might say, 'Girlfriend, that's life! People die everyday.' Yeah, I guess you are right. Getting on with life does seem to be the norm, even if it means we just muddle through it. I am now convinced, however, that slowing down or simply pausing at such times is crucial. In doing so, we ensure that we do not become ensnared by our difficult life experiences. This pause, in the midst of it all, gives us the opportunity to stop holding our breath – and simply breathe.

When I recommend breathing space, I am not talking about locking ourselves away, as doing so jeopardises our wellbeing and development. It is about giving ourselves permission to press the pause button. And why not? We are happy to make concessions for physical illness so why shouldn't we when it comes to matters of the heart and soul.

A result of not finding a healthy balance, not knowing when to take time out, is that we can flee into our 'castles', get trapped – and never find the 'right' keys to get out. Not knowing any other way to handle the situation we remain there helpless. Some of us want to get out but do not know how; others may want to come out, and need to do so – but dare not, for the risk of being hurt.

What I have learned is that while we cannot completely avoid heartache or pain on this side of heaven, we can learn how to move past them to maintain a healthy heart.

Old issues, modern castles

We have established that very few of us (if any) are able to lock ourselves away in castles indefinitely. To some extent we have to get on with the stuff of life. However, it is still possible to hide from others, to lock ourselves away mentally and spiritually.

So how can one tell?

Well, once the doors are slammed shut, the first thing we endeavour to do is make ourselves feel safe and comfortable in our new surroundings and we swiftly adapt to our 'people-less' world.

So here you are, you modern princess you! Whilst poor Princess Leanne had to make do with her own company, you may not be as bored as she was. Thank God for the likes of television, radio, computers, books, iPads (and the entire Apple family), smart phones, game consoles (where you can play games and sports or join in activities or fitness programmes. You can play by yourself or with a virtual partner – and you get your own virtual instructors and cheerleaders). With all this, you might think you are set for life. You could have a cardio workout without setting your foot in the gym. You can go bowling or play tennis without leaving your front room. You can have a party – all by yourself – with music, dancing, food and drink. You can learn a skill such as cooking, typing, or learning a foreign language – all through your computer or electronic device. You can watch re-runs of your favourite programmes, broadcast from around the world, or watch movies – back to back – online. You can buy your groceries, or pretty much anything you fancy, without having to traipse up and down aisles of a supermarket or go into town. You can get lost in surfing the internet aimlessly for hours – going from one site to another.

It seems that technology has enabled us to have a happy life. Can this be true? I don't think so. Whilst it may seem that people are doing well, hopping from site to site, they can do it all without anyone else being on the scene. I do not believe this was ever the web's intended purpose but it has come to serve many people who have, consciously or not, cut others from their lives. And whilst it may seem like they are doing well, the original issue that caused them to put up barriers still remains.

You can even take it a notch higher. Unlike Princess Leanne, you do not even need to sit on your royal balcony to watch what people are doing. With Facebook and other social media tools you can catch up with what is going on in other people's lives through their status updates and discussions. You can view photos of their vacations, children's birthdays, reunions, and watch them having fun with others. You see what is going on – from the balcony of your royal castle.

You live in a community that consists of you, and no one else. You might argue that you are not living on planet Lonely: you still go to work, pop to the gym, attend church, and meet with friends and family. But the truth is that although you may be surrounded by people something is still amiss. Look closely and you will notice how you have been keeping people at arm's length. They can only get so far with you and no further. You have not opted to lock yourself away in a physical sense – but your heart is under lock and key and others have no access to it.

And you have become a 'pro' at this. Your body shows up but your heart is kept at a safe distance. It has been hurt, wounded or broken once before and you are not about to put it on a platter to be hurt again. After all, that would be foolish, right? You figure that if are going to safeguard your heart you had better set the rules – the terms of your relationships. You decide how close other people can get. You decide how much you reveal.

If you were betrayed by a friend, you decide never trust others – much less confide in them.

If you have been hurt in a relationship with a guy, you decree that no man shall ever hurt you again, as Lola and Krista did.

If you were trodden on by colleagues in their scramble to progress, you too decide to tread on others if that is what it takes – after all, everyone else is doing it.

After having been in a joint business venture with a trusted colleague that went sour, you decide to fly solo.

In fact, flying solo seems to be your mantra these days – but your stance is underpinned with difficult emotions, such as bitterness, resentment, lack of forgiveness, anger, frustration, and more. Which are your 'wicked dragon' experiences that contributed to the trapped princess we see in you today?

Which strategies are you using when you deal with people? Have you learned to keep your heart hidden when you are with them? Do you rely on modern techie tools to keep you busy and create an illusion of being in the thick of it? If you do, then you are buying into what I call a 'modern day deception' – one that keeps us trapped and perpetuates our original issues. It covers over our true state (i.e. wounded), hinders our growth, and prolongs our trauma.

I admire independence and the ability to make do for ourselves when we are genuinely cut off from friends or family for reasons of geographical location, unrelenting work demands, or personal commitments. However, it is also possible to choose to use these 'reasons' as a way of keeping others from us.

We need to take a long, hard look at what we are doing. When we catch ourselves choosing not to answer phone calls, or find ourselves texting, sending emails, or 'poking' someone on Facebook rather than making a date to meet in the flesh, we need to be completely honest with ourselves. Only then can we embrace the truth behind our attitudes, beliefs and behaviours. My question to you is this: is there a Princess Leanne lurking in you somewhere?

If you can relate to what you have read so far, I think now is an appropriate time to move on to the issues that sent you hiding. Your story does not have to end as Princess Leanne's did. You can write your own ending, regardless of what happened at the beginning – and make it a happy one. Just remember: you do not have to remain barricaded away from people and, ultimately, life.

Chapter Two

A tale of two princesses

Whenever I write a book, I do my utmost to help the reader absorb the subject matter so that they not only understand the generic problem I am describing but also gain an understanding of how the problem may relate to themselves. The story of Princess Leanne is a simple fable designed to raise the reader's own self-awareness. The 'wicked dragon' is a symbol which represents 'traumatic experience'. I chose Leanne because I recognized that her situation will be recognized by many women; her problem is one that many others face. Now we will look at two other princesses.

The beautiful flower that closed up for good

As I was pondering about what to include in this section of the book, the sad story of Tamar, from the Bible, came to mind. This time we have a tale of a real princess, the daughter of the great King David, a story which reveals what can happen to an open, tender, innocent heart as a result of some extraordinarily hurtful experiences.

Tamar is a flower blossoming beautifully in her father's house. Let us just imagine her waking up happy each day – just a typical young woman, without a care in the world. She is interested in looking her best – fixing her hair, wearing her royal robes and jewellery – and being with her family and friends. She has so much going for her and her future looks bright.

Then Tamar is raped.

The story in *2 Samuel 13* reveals that her half-brother, Amnon, had taken a lustful fancy to Tamar. Rather than asking the king for her hand, Amnon and his cousin Jonadab planned how to lure Tamar to his private quarters. They decided that Amnon should fake an illness and when his father would come to visit him, Amnon would ask if his half-sister, Tamar, could be sent over to his house and allowed to cook his favourite dish. David, the unsuspecting father, agreed to this and sent Tamar to Amnon's house. Then, after Tamar had prepared the food, Amnon requested that she feed him in his bedroom. It was there that Amnon raped Tamar, ignoring her pleas. After he had had his way with her, her half-brother's love turned to hate. He told her to leave and when she tried to plead with him not to turn her out of his house, he got one of his servants to throw her out. Amnon compounded his sin when he treated Tamar like a cheap piece of meat. To her, the rape was cruel enough, but abandoning her afterwards was even worse.

Here is what happened after Tamar's ordeal:

¹⁸⁻¹⁹ *She was wearing a long-sleeved gown. [That is how virgin princesses used to dress from early adolescence.] Tamar poured ashes on her head, then she ripped the long-sleeved gown, held her head in her hands, and walked away, sobbing as she went.*

²⁰ *Her brother Absalom said to her, 'Has your brother Amnon had his way with you? Now, my dear sister, let's keep it quiet – a family matter. He is, after all, your brother. Don't take this so hard.' Tamar lived in her brother Absalom's home, bitter and desolate.*

2 Samuel 13: 18–20 (MSG)

First she poured ashes on her head. Then she tore off the clothes that represented her purity and heritage feeling there was no use for them as she was no longer a virgin. Sobbing, she headed for the house of her older brother, Absalom, who tries to comfort her. However, he also gave her gagging orders, asking her to keep the matter quiet. As it was her brother who did this to her they needed to hush the whole thing up – it was a family matter.

This story is thousands of years old and yet elements of it are so topical today. I will not, in this book, attempt to explore the reasons we try to cover up atrocities in our society, whether they are in the home, office, church or other places of worship, or the community at large. We know that countless women suffer in silence. Rather, I would like to focus on how Tamar dealt with her trauma – which I suspect may shine a light on how women today, suffering violent experiences, deal with their own.

In Tamar we have a young, beautiful, confident, virgin princess – with a healthy dose of self-esteem – who was reduced to a depressed recluse after the rape. We are told only that Tamar remained in Absalom's house after the incident, a bitter and desolate woman. Again, we can use our imaginations to picture her life there: her brother Absalom knocking on her bedroom door, inviting her to join them for the family meal, and being sent away. Though people may have tried to get access to Tamar's heart, the drawbridge was up – possibly for good.

Although we do not know what happened to Tamar next, let us make some inferences:

- She never got over her rape ordeal, nor was there any indication that she had support from others to help her deal with it.

- Been forced to keep silent about the matter meant Tamar had no means of opening up to others and expressing how she felt.

- Although she learned that her father had heard about the rape, we do not hear of him visiting her (as he did when he heard Amnon was unwell). Tamar would have taken his silence to mean that he did not care about her, or that being a girl-child meant she was insignificant.

- Tamar would have felt that justice had not been served and she would have felt helpless with no advocate to fight on her behalf.

- In her shame, Tamar felt the only thing she could do was to withdraw from others. That way, she would not have to confront her perpetrator on festival days, or family events. And, that way, she would not have to be reminded of the horrible ordeal every time she saw Amnon; nor would she be forced to play 'happy families' when she was harbouring bitterness in her heart. By hiding herself away, she could keep her heart from being damaged further.

- As a result of the rape, Tamar never married. She had to carry the stigma and shame of no longer being a virgin after her ordeal. Virginity was something to be prized. Who would want her now? What was the point now in her caring for her appearance? And the bitterest cut of all: in never being able to have a husband of her own, she would have no children.

Is it any surprise that our beautiful flower closed up for good?

As in Tamar's story, some of us are sent fleeing into our own castles where we shut ourselves away from the world. There we find some form of sanctuary from the storms of life. However, we are the daughters of a Great King, God, and in doing so we are choosing to live below the standards He has set for us, and we are wilfully excluding ourselves from experiencing the privileges of being a royal princess.

Journaling Moment

In Princess Leanne's case, it was the wicked dragon that sent her into hiding. In Tamar's case, it was her rape ordeal at the hand of her half-brother. What situation in life has sent you fleeing into your castle and slamming the door shut?

Me, God and no one else!

'But that's the way God created me!'

The next princess I would like to mention is *me*! If you thought I would write a book on something I have not experienced you were wrong! I have found, as with my other books, that God uses them to promote restoration, healing and growth in the lives of the readers as well as the writer. So I have boldly included a snippet of my life – a period when I too lived as a trapped princess – a period that was to end when God decided to chuck me out of my 'castle' and bring me in line to experience His idea of real living.

Firstly, I want to share with you a fact that I discovered – one which surprised but enlightened me. My default personality type, I found out, is more towards the introvert end of the scale than extrovert. (And I have the test results to prove it!) According to the work of Carl Jung (a psychologist), an introvert can be seen as someone who is introspective, prefers solitary activities over social ones, and can work more productively when alone. It is not the same thing as being shy: shy people avoid social encounters out of fear – and they may, indeed be extroverts. Instead, introverts tend to prefer fewer social activities. Introversion and extroversion are the opposite ends of a continuum (as opposed to two sides of a coin). This means all of us will find ourselves at different points along it.

Personality types are never purely one thing or another. Although I am more towards the introvert end of the scale, I do have some extrovert attributes. My introvert tendencies would explain why open-plan offices, with decibels of noise and tons of activity in the background, never work for me. In that environment, I simply cannot think – much less work. Moreover, it stifles my creative juices. In the past, when I have had to work in that kind of place, I would find myself slinking away to a peaceful spot – whether it was my car or an empty office – to find some peace and sanity. Without creating a pause, every now and then, in situations of intense noise and activity, I find I cannot function effectively and find it overwhelming.

We all create coping strategies, and I have come to realise that my creativity, effectiveness, productivity and performance rests on this one of mine. I need to put systems in place, proactively, to accommodate my own particular needs. *It is who I am*. Moreover, I have come to accept that the person God has created me to be is perfectly suited to my primary calling (namely writing).

That said, the extrovert in me yearns to come out to play every so often and I find I have to monitor the introvert in me, consciously and proactively, so that I can make the necessary adjustment from time to time.

Me + God − people = good ...?

Being an introvert, I find that when I am faced with a new opportunity or challenge −or if I feel pressured − it is natural for me to retreat inwardly and pull away from others. I need this time to think, reflect, pray, regroup and re-strategise. And, as a result of my 'me time' − which could last anything from a few moments to a few days − I feel ready to tackle whatever I am faced with.

However, when I am faced with my own 'wicked dragon' moments, my 'think-reflect-pray-regroup-re-strategise' rationale is instantly skewed. It goes into overdrive and I want to flee for dear life. Like Princess Leanne, I find myself retreating into my castle and staying there for longer periods of time than are healthy. During such times, I feel a false sense of safety behind the bolted drawbridge of my heart. And with access denied to anyone to the deepest places of my heart, I feel no one can hurt me there.

When this has happened in the past, I ask myself: was this introversion flipped on its head or has it gone to an extreme? I don't know. But what I do know is that I found a sense of safety and comfort in my castle. Of course, I still worked, attended church, and did all the normal everyday stuff − except the fact that my heart was kept hidden in a safe place to avoid further hurt. And while I created the space to lick my wounds, they never *really* got healed. At the time, retreating into my 'castle' and putting up the drawbridge was the only way I knew to handle such moments. And so I embraced it.

Life in the castle was not all bad. In fact, I made myself comfortable. The prospect of staying there forever was almost exciting, in the way a child gets excited when they are about to discover a new adventure. I thought, 'I could really live like this.' I even spiritualised it by saying, 'It's just me and You, Lord' – which made me feel deep and spiritual because, after all, I was walking with God every day without annoying human interferences (which were kept to a minimum).

My formula for living was as follows:

Me + God – People = Good

Me + God + People = Not So Good

The second equation expressed was not working for me. Bringing people into it equated to hard work which only ever seemed to end up in pain and hurt. Yes, I did have, and still maintain, a number of relationships. However, looking back, I realise that, as a result of some hurtful past experiences, I struggled to yield my heart fully. Many relationships only went as deep as I allowed them to go. And some – those which I considered 'high risk' – were kept at arm's length. You see, trusting others can be a big issue for introverts – they find trust is hard to repair once damaged. And, looking back, I can honestly say that those were the days I had lost faith and trust in the human race.

How God started me on my journey

That was the bubble I lived in for a while. Then, one day, I felt God burst it by telling me: 'You can't have Me without the church.' I felt annoyed – almost betrayed –

at first by His lack of understanding.

I knew that by 'church' He was referring to both the body of Christ and people in general and that God was telling me that He was wanting me, expecting me, to engage fully with people again. As I was nursing a long list of hurts that spanned back to my childhood days, I was distraught that the one Person I thought would understand my plight was now causing chaos in my 'happy' world. The prospect of letting the drawbridge down and jeopardising my safety was daunting. Stepping out meant becoming vulnerable to hurt again. It meant confronting your wicked dragons. And here God was, nudging me back into deep, meaningful and loving relationships with others. My days in the castle – home sweet home – were coming to an end and I did not like the feeling one bit. But I could not ignore what was happening: I could feel Him tugging on my heart, gently and insistently, telling me, 'It's time to get back out there.'

I could have pulled the 'introvert' card on God, reminding Him that it was He who had made me this way. What I did do was reel out my long list of hurts and the reasons why I should be granted an indefinite stay in my castle, but it was of no use. His mind was made up and I was served my notice to quit the property. He knew that the way I was living was not sustainable in the long term. The battle was lost: I only had to glance through His Word to realise that whilst He accepts me, warts 'n' all, He does expect me to abide by His rules, principles and standards – all which I recognise are for my own good. He has my best interests at heart.

Most significantly, He sent me to the very rules and principles I was running away from, and it made me feel like a modern-day Jonah. Jonah had got in a boat and fled in the opposite direction from where his duty lay, and I recognised that I had been doing the same with my heart and had embarked on a journey God did not desire for me.

Reluctantly, I conceded God had a point. I knew it was a truth I had to face, sooner or later. And despite my being in the castle, I had to acknowledge that not much had gone on in the healing department. All I had achieved was create time and space to relive my hurt, over and over again. I was caught in a trap and could not break loose without His help. The great thing about God is that He always provides the means of escape and He knows just what to do to help me heal. And He gave me the steps I needed to take to let down the drawbridge of my heart again.

That all happened a while back. God graciously and lovingly got me on my journey of restoration and reconciliation. I will go into much more detail as to the 'how' later in this book but I will say this – one of the things He did was to bring into my life some amazingly loving and supportive people. Some were new, whilst others were people I already knew. And the amazing thing about this God-ordained move was that they were already positioned by my drawbridge, patiently waiting for me to let it down. He set up the whole thing: mobilising not only me, but the people who would demonstrate His love for me.

God was never in denial of the fact that I had been hurt. He knew everything that had gone on up to the point when I fled into my castle. And knowing how fragile I was, and the struggles I would have faced reintegrating myself – or rather my heart – with society, He prepared the ground – did the leg work to help me. He set everything up in order for me to be healed of my wounded heart. As for my role? I had to be willing, and find the courage, to step out of my place of hiding. When I did so, I was overwhelmed by my supporters' demonstration of God's love. I am *still* amazed how unconditionally loving some people can be – which serves as a constant reminder of Gods unconditional love towards me. Amazing!

When the time came to unbolt the doors to my heart, I asked Father to help me *really* and *truly* get over past hurts and learn how to enjoy a relationship with others – to get over my experiences, personality traits, attitudes, beliefs and behaviours. And one day, when it seemed my heart was ready, Father asked me to start a study on healing from hurts and learning to trust others again. I was not expecting to have to do this (in fact, I was hoping for something rather dramatic, such as His patting my head and downloading all the new attitudes, beliefs and behaviours I would need. Or even his putting me to sleep so that, lo and behold, by the time I woke up it turned out to be nothing more than a dream). But oh no! Father told me to get up, and make notes of those things He brought to my heart.

My writing was to serve as an aide memoire for me and His other daughters who were trapped in castles of their own. This book comprises the key themes and lessons I learnt on my way. Maybe you have found yourself locked up in a castle of your own? Maybe you feel it is time to deal with the hurtful situations you have faced? Or it could be that you want to let down the drawbridge of your castle but do not know how. Wherever you are at today, God can help. It may seem daunting but I am living proof that with God, 'all things are indeed possible' (*Luke 1:37*). And all I ask from you is a receptive heart. I pray you experience healing of your wounds and restoration from your plight. May Father speak into your heart, as He did mine, and show you the way to living the abundant life – as He planned it.

But before we delve into learning how to unlock the drawbridges of our hearts, let us look at some of the characteristics of a trapped princess.

Chapter Three

Discovering the trapped princess in you

f you have ever read any of my other books, such as *Healing a Discouraged Heart: Getting Back on Track When Life Lets You Down* and *Overcoming Emotional Baggage: A Woman's Guide to Living the Abundant Life*, you will know that I like to include sections that paint a picture, attempting that way to depict how the subject of the book might be described through characters and events in everyday life. In *Overcoming Emotional Baggage*, I described ten female 'hybrid' types, each carrying emotional baggage, with whom other women could identify. In *Healing A Discouraged Heart* I talk about the many faces of discouragement, and these are exemplified in the lives of four people I describe.

I use these scenes and pictures to raise your own self-awareness. Oftentimes, when reading a book, we can fall into the trap of separating ourselves from the issue being discussed. If only I had a penny for every woman I have come across who declares, 'I have no baggage.' But when I go on to describe what 'baggage' looks like in everyday scenarios, hey presto! – they realise they have plenty of it. Denial can blind us, so beware!

In this chapter I will list a variety of traits which may well feel familiar to you. Hopefully, they will help you to become more self-aware.

Enlightening Moment

Don't be perturbed by or hung up on what you discover. Rather, accept it and be determined to move on by taking the necessary action.

Common traits of hurting, trapped princesses

So what are the traits of a trapped princess?

I am hoping that the tale of Princess Leanne, the story of Tamar, and my personal experience has started to shed some light as to what a trapped princess looks like.

You might not have iron bars on your windows, or a drawbridge replacing the doors to your home or room, but we both know there is a barrier you have put up with a 'no entry' sign to the doorway to your heart.

So how can you tell if you have become a trapped princess? Below are some tell-tale signs I have come across. Please note this is *not* an exhaustive list. Neither is it a psychological test. It is what it is: a list of some traits, attitudes, beliefs and behaviours I have discovered over the years.

Social traits

- You prefer to be on your own most of the time even when you have the opportunity to be around others.

- You have no friends in those places you frequent often, e.g. church, work, gym.

- You avoid building relationships with people, especially deep and meaningful ones.

- You take on a persona when you are around people in a bid to deflect any hint of your wounded heart.

- You hide behind a mask (e.g. busyness, success, appearance) so that people do not get to see the real you – in particular, the wounded you.

- You use social media as a means to keep people at a distance, or away.

- You turn down invitations and find reasons to avoid others.

- You allow few or no visitors into your personal space. You have decided how far they can come.

- You agree to meet others but, more often than not, find reasons to 'chicken out' at the last minute, as the idea makes you feel anxious.

- You tend to be suspecting of people around you – most often for no real reason.

- You are convinced that people are out there to hurt you so you keep them at arm's length.

- You are detached, socially and emotionally, from others – though they may be physically in close proximity (e.g. in work or living situations).

- You cannot remember the last time you poured out your heart to others because you have not allowed anyone close enough to do so.

- When people try to come close, you push them away – consciously or not. It could be in your words or body language.

- You have few real friends – if any at all. The friendships you do have, you do not invest in so that the relationship eventually dwindles.

- You get irritated by people. They just get on your nerves.

- You find yourself hiding from love or platonic relationships as you believe they could hurt you.

- You wish you knew how to reach out to others to allow them back into your world, but you simply do not know how.

- When people are nice to you, you suspect instantly that they might want something from you.

- You avoid people or situations that remind you of your hurtful experiences.

Emotional and mental traits

- You tend to see people as the 'enemy', as your outlook is clouded by your past or present experiences.

- You find yourself crying a lot. At times, it is because of your hurts. At other times, you just do not know why.

- You experience bouts of depression and/or have had suicidal thoughts.

- Despite the passing of time, certain memories, objects, people, or places still trigger a negative response in you. For example, someone's name may be mentioned which has you instantly spitting venom.

- You experience feelings of emptiness, isolation and loneliness.

- You find yourself becoming anxious when faced the possibility of getting 'close' to people.

- You avoid anything that might bring about intimacy.

- Your heart has been wounded and/or broken from previous experience(s) and you just cannot get over it.

- You have recurring dreams or nightmares. Their themes tend to be related to your hurtful experience(s).

- You have developed negative coping behaviours to keep your 'boat' afloat, such as using food, alcohol, drugs, busyness, or money. (These act as a temporary filler to numb your pain and provide a means of escape from the realities of your world.)

- You keep having flashbacks of your traumatic experience(s).

- You find yourself emotionally numb to people and/or situations.

- You throw yourself into excessive or addictive behaviour to take your mind off things.

- You self-harm.

- You struggle to connect with others emotionally because of your issues with trust and your fear of being hurt.

- Your self-esteem and self-confidence have taken a nosedive.

- You tend to have negative attitudes towards people and life in general.

- You use daydreaming or fantasizing to escape the pain of your real world or to create your ideal world. This may lead to your talking to yourself (audibly or in your head).

- You know you are trapped, emotionally, but feel hopeless and helpless about the situation.

- You are nursing negative emotions, such as hatred, bitterness, guilt, lack of forgiveness, or resentment.

- You find yourself apportioning blame, regarding your painful experience, to yourself or others.

- You relive your painful experience constantly. Your mind replays how you were hurt over and over again, so much so that you cannot switch it off.

- You do not feel strong enough to confront people who have hurt you (it could be due to their position/status, role, location, etc.). As a result, you find yourself lashing out at other people.

- You wish secretly that bad things would happen to those who caused you pain. When you hear that they have suffered some woe or other, you are secretly happy or feel numb.

- You bad-mouth those who have hurt you.

- You find yourself saying, 'I'm never going to let that happen to me again', and you put things into place to ensure that 'it' never happens again.

- You feel so traumatised by the way you were treated, that you constantly struggle with the thought: 'how could they do this to me?'.

- Over time, your perception of what really took place has become skewed. You find yourself filling the gaps with untruths or increasing the gravity of the issue (particularly when the issue is relatively minor).

- Because you do not have access to those who hurt you, you create imaginary scenarios where you tell offenders exactly how you feel.

- You are no longer passionate about life. Your outlook tends to be pessimistic.

- You feel the whole world is out to get you.

- You have been hurt by the fact that those who should know better abused your trust and hurt you the most.

Spiritual traits

- You are struggling with a lack of forgiveness towards those who hurt you.

- You are finding it difficult to pray, in general, or bring the hurtful situation(s) to God.

- You have issues with God. In your mind, God could have averted the hurtful situation or saved you from it. But, as far as you are concerned, He chose not to.

- You feel unloved and forgotten by God and others.

- You feel guilty for the way you have been feeling. You may feel you should have handled matters better or have responded differently.

- You claim to have forgiven those who have hurt you verbally but it has not reached your heart yet.

- You are in denial about how wounded your heart really is: your strategy has been to bury your head in the sand and pretend to others, and yourself, that everything is fine. Deep down, though, you know that is not the case.

- You feel no one understands the pain you are feeling. This can include God as well as others.

- Though you have tried to open up to God and/ or others, you find the experience too painful, so you just clam up.

Elizabeth

These spiritual traits were pretty much how Elizabeth (the ex-wife of John, a Chief Executive of a global firm) felt. Five years after her divorce, after discovering he had had a series of extra-marital affairs throughout their marriage – one of which resulted in a child being conceived – the hurt and pain still raged through Elizabeth's heart. What hurt her the most was the fact that she had given up a lucrative career twenty-two years ago to build their home whilst John built his own successfully as the main breadwinner. After those years of unswerving loyalty, she felt utterly betrayed and humiliated.

Elizabeth had been raised in the Christian faith and knew that God would have wanted her to forgive John – but how could she even begin to forgive a man who had hurt her so badly? She started to vent her frustrations at God: where was God when all this was going on? Didn't He care? Didn't any of her prayers count for anything? Where was God when she was hurting? Such thoughts kept Elizabeth away from church as she could not reconcile her faith with her hurts. Her experiences had all but put out the once raging fires of her heart – and the remnants of her faith.

Other traits

Whilst you may not pour ashes on your head or rip your clothes off, as Tamar did in the Bible, here is what you might do:

- You withdraw from activities and passions that you once considered fun, ones which you found fulfilling and that contributed to your sense of wellbeing.

- You make yourself comfortable living in your castle and adapt to that. You convince yourself you do not need anyone else and find ways to cope in your isolated world.

- You change something about yourself that makes you unreachable, e.g. move away, change numbers, take on attitudes others find difficult to handle, or adopt socially-unacceptable behaviours.

- When out of your castle, you feel like a fish out of water and cannot wait to get back into your comfort zone. When back in, you breathe a sigh of relief.

- You do not pay attention to how you look and let yourself go, something you would never have done in the past. This can include your hair, appearance, clothes, weight, health, personal hygiene, etc.

- You do something drastic such as cutting off all your hair.

- Your wounded heart and hurtful experiences have started to affect one or more aspects of your everyday life, such as your career, finances, etc.

Again, this is not an exhaustive list. But if many of the items on it are familiar to you, it is a good indicator that all may not be well in your world. (One must also remember that there are plenty of unavoidable life situations that may trigger some of these responses, making us feel isolated and lonely. These include working away from home, relocating, a promotion, dealing with ill-health, and even getting married or having a child. So it pays to consider your personal circumstances before jumping to any conclusions.)

Journaling Moment

You might be able to relate to one or more of these traits. The trick is to consider the driving force behind your actions. So ask yourself the following:

- What are my motives?

- Why do I do the things I do? (In the context of hiding from people.)

- Are my attitudes, beliefs and behaviours as a result of one or more hurtful life situations?

- Do I have any unresolved issues I need to be dealing with?

As you make your way through these indicators, watch out that you do not exclude yourself from the equation. Trapped princesses come in all shapes, sizes and walks of life. They do not all live alone and/or are single! BIG MISCONCEPTION! Some are married, live with friends or parents, have children, share a house, care for others, lead organisations or run businesses; they may be politicians or even celebrities. They do not necessarily cut themselves off from civilisation and live on Planet Mars! If you think the typical princess trapped in her own world is a Billy-no-mates or a geeky-looking lady with a warped sense of fashion, think again! A trapped woman is a much more subtle thing. Remember Princess Leanne? She looked the bomb – but her heart was hurting.

The only true test is what I call your 'Heart Test'. Your heart holds the truth even though you may endeavour to lie to yourself. The Heart Test is about looking at what is driving your attitudes, beliefs and behaviours. Is what you do motivated by love, hate, lack of forgiveness, anger, or the hurts of yesterday or yesteryears? Only you can answer that. And do not be fooled by appearances: it is what is going on inside that really counts.

Think carefully before you jump to the conclusion: 'that's how God made me!' You will remember that that was my reaction when I found moving out of my 'castle' an uncomfortable prospect. I urge caution when using such statements: we tend to think this way when we are nudged to confront our issues – as a cop-out – so that we can continue to bury our heads in the sand and live in denial. If this is where you are at, you may benefit from reading my second book: *Overcoming Emotional Baggage: A Woman's Guide to Living the Abundant Life.*

Journaling Moment

Conduct your own Heart Test: take a moment to revisit the list of traits and, in the spirit of honesty, ask God to help you see what you may have missed. Which may apply to you? Can you construct your own list of traits?

Understanding how your body responds

Mysterious problems

Recently, I read the book: *Sick and Tired: Healing Diseases Doctors Can't Cure* by Dr Nick Read. All I can say is, 'I KNEW IT!' 'Knew what?' you ask.

Our unresolved issues can cause a barrage of physical symptoms and ailments. The mind-body link has long been established, and there are many books on the subject, but on reading Dr Read's book, which pulls together decades of research, I had a eureka moment.

Many of us have found ourselves traipsing to our GPs where we have listed a number of symptoms. Yet, frustratingly, after tests and countless trips to see consultants have been made, there is no straight-forward medical explanation as to what is causing the very real symptoms we are experiencing. And so, after ruling out all the obvious illnesses, GPs are left scratching their heads, wondering what could be causing their patients the muscle aches, constipation, diarrhoea, chronic fatigue, headaches, tremors, and much more. These 'functional diseases', as Dr Read calls them, are clearly real enough for the patient. When he looked at the details of his own patients' symptoms he was convinced that none of the sufferers was a hypochondriac.

After many years of being baffled, this determined doctor – who was also a qualified psychotherapist – began to unravel the truth. In asking his patients about their life circumstances and experiences, especially those which happened around the time their symptoms started, he noticed an important correlation. For many, their physical problems started at a time when they had faced a major personal challenge or trauma.

Dr Read also noticed that some individuals were experiencing symptoms not as a direct result of a current situation, but triggered as a response to a previous situation – one that may have taken place years before, often in childhood. He went on to explain that when we face a situation similar to one that we have had to deal with in the past, our bodies remember how we reacted to the previous situation and simply replicate the response.

Let us just imagine – as an example – that you were bullied in school and no one wanted to play with you in the playground. It was your first experience of bullying and rejection. At the time, in your unhappiness, you had a tummy ache and felt sick when you tried to eat anything. Now, years on, here you are as an adult. You are finding it difficult at work: there is a new boss and she is on your back the whole time and you find it hard to stand up to her. You find yourself experiencing exactly the same symptoms you felt as a child. Not only that, but you remember how nauseous you felt when your boyfriend dumped you the previous year. You found it almost impossible to eat anything, and your stomach was in knots.

Your body remembers its responses to previous traumatic situations. If you manage a difficult situation proactively – talking the problem through with someone and seeking help – the physical response will be less acute. However, if you internalise the experience you are likely feel those symptoms all over again. Being conscious and proactive is all important.

Failure to forgive

Recently, a good friend of mine, Sharon Platt-McDonald (Director of Health, Disability & Women Ministries, British Union Conference of The Seventh-day Adventist UK), wrote a wonderful book called, *Extending The Olive Branch: Forgiveness As Healing* (ISBN: 978-0-95666290-1-2). After decades in the healthcare sector herself, alongside extensive research, she stated the following:

> *'Medical science now demonstrates the harmful effects of choosing not to forgive and holding on to resentments. Amongst the emerging evidence researchers have presented is data suggesting that failure to forgive could over a lifetime raise a person's risk for heart disease, mental illness and other debilitating illnesses. Some studies have suggested that forgiveness actually improves health.'*

She goes on to say that,

> *'Historically, forgiveness has been at the heart of the teachings of major religions. Yet empirical research from clinical and social psychologists, medical practitioners and other researchers is producing evidence demonstrating the link between the emotions and heart health.'*

So, it seems that the *state of our heart affects our heart!* By this, I simply mean that the 'stuff' we carry about with us, as a result of our being hurt, can cause problems with our physical heart, as well as our general health. This is just one part of the extensive amount of research that shows a link between the mind and illness.

Another book, *"The Hidden Cause of High Blood Pressure: How to find the right treatment"* by Dr Samuel J. Mann (ISBN: 072253678X) challenges the notion that an increase in blood pressure comes as a result of times of stress, tension, anger and anxiety. Through his research, Dr Mann believes that there are deeper and hidden causes, such as problems from childhood and blocked emotions, that we perhaps do not factor in. Whilst we have come to associate the illness with 'hyper'-type people, his findings highlight the fact that those of us who appear to be calm whilst keeping a lid on our feelings, without any outlet for them, were the ones in real danger.

As a result of such important research which continues to find a strong mind-body link in illness, medical professionals will have to tilt towards a more holistic approach. As Dr Nick Read suggests, physicians (and, indeed, ourselves) need to consider our life 'stories' when trying to treat us.

There is no doubt in my mind that if we are to remain in 'Princess Leanne' mode, we will face a raft of physical symptoms and challenges. This is a compelling reason for us to come out of hiding and deal with our unresolved issues so as not to end up with a barrage of physical issues.

The penny drops

The stories Dr Read recounted that jumped out at me the most were the ones where patients were experiencing digestive disorders, constipation in particular (which had been a bugbear for me in the past). The symptom tended to arise as a result of an individual not having an opportunity to open up about their experiences or get support in overcoming them. If you clam up, it seems the body can do likewise. When a person does not get the opportunity to share their experiences, or they do not feel safe enough to open up, or they feel they are not being 'heard' their digestive systems can clam up with constipation.

Why this resonates with me? Because I had never made the connection between what was going on in my wounded heart – at the time I was a 'trapped princess' – with my temperamental bowels. When I clammed up and retreated ... guess what? They did the same! The gradual realisation – a growing consciousness – of the link between the state of my heart and soul and my body was what ultimately sorted the physical problem. But this awareness took a long time to come as I was focusing on external factors.

Lorna and Jennifer

Lorna – a middle aged professional – had shared that she almost always suffered with bowel issues when she was experiencing problems in her troubled marriage. Her strategy had always been to keep her head down and say nothing, hoping they would all blow over – including her husbands controlling and overbearing tendencies – but her body was suffering as a consequence.

Jennifer, on the other hand, who is a close friend of Lorna, had no problem vocalising her feelings. She was often known to fly into tantrums when frustrated with her relationships, especially with her estranged mother, who had showed up after 35 years, wanting to pick up where she left off (after abandoning her at the age of five). During such emotional displays, Jennifer would find herself running to the bathroom with bouts of diarrhoea and stomach cramps.

The interesting fact in Lorna's and Jennifer's cases was that they had been, for quite some time, completely unaware of the link between their physical symptoms and their personal stories. We need to make these links – and doing so can make an important starting point of our journeys to experience freedom from past hurts.

Before I became aware of the mind-body link, I had felt increasingly frustrated. I spent hours searching the internet, trying to self-diagnose or self-medicate, and yet nothing was helping. Then, in my frustration, I started praying about it. You might think that, being a Christian, that this would have been my first point of call. It was … kinda. You know how it is when you throw your prayers out there and say general statements such as, 'Lord, heal me'? Well, I had been doing that. But, while this is a good start, we usually need to get much more specific, and start digging a little deeper.

It was only when I had put aside my obsessive researching and quietened my ever-inquisitive mind and turned to God instead of the internet that I started getting somewhere. I started to ask questions like: 'Why do I feel like this?', 'What is the real cause?', 'What can I do to resolve it?' I needed God, through the Holy Spirit, to reveal what was *really* going on. I needed to be enlightened about the things I could not see for myself. And this is where the journey to healing started – when I *really* desired to dig deep and face the underlying problem ... no matter how painful it was.

And just in case you are wondering, this did not happen overnight. I did say it was a journey, and quite rightly so. God loved me too much to overwhelm me and He knew what I could handle. So the journey lasted for a while. Moreover, He used a range of tools that included books (Christian and secular), the Scriptures (of course), movies, lectures/sermons, my dreams, someone else's experiences, and another person sharing a spiritual insight – all underpinned by the Holy Spirit who would ever so kindly and gently shine His torch into my troubled heart and soul.

Through this process, the eyes of my understanding became more and more open. I became more self-aware – awakened to what was lurking beneath the surface, a problem which I had been carrying around for ages. At first, I wondered why God did not simply part the clouds and use His heavenly megaphone to shout out from Heaven, 'Gladys, you got baggage, girl. Deal with it!' Why was I oblivious to the real me? I feel part of the problem rested in the fact that I put all my energies and focus into mask-wearing and withdrawing from others; I felt a compelling need to hide for self-preservation. And in doing so, I could not see the entire jigsaw puzzle of my life.

I am sure my body must have got confused over the years. I can just hear it talking with my soul and spirit, over a cup of coffee, in frustration:

> *'Here, you two, I'm kinda confused. Here she is crying all night, having withdrawn from others, and comfort-eating like it's going out of fashion – yet every morning she acts like everything is OK and expects me to go along with that. I just don't get her! And whilst I am trying to figure her out, I get confused as to what should be my next move. Should I fight, take flight, or just shut down. I was never taught how to handle this in Body School. Any ideas, folks?'*

And so the cycle continued every time life kicked me in the gut. I hid away – and my gut bore the brunt of the pain. Yet, I marvel at Gods patience and mercy. He took me on a journey of healing to the point where I can now write to you and share some of what I learned.

I included this section intentionally so that you could add it to your checklist. And if you have unexplained physical symptoms which have left your doctor scratching his/her head, before you go off to 'bind the devil' or resort to further medical intervention, ask God to help you search your heart. (Please note, I am not knocking either of these as they have their place.) But first, consider *your story* – your personal journey to date. What has been happening in your world that may be having a negative impact on your body? Are there any niggling symptoms that you have not been able to shift or resolve – even with your best efforts and external interventions? It is worth reflecting on.

Journaling Moment

Write down your story. How have you reacted to it? How has it affected you – spirit, soul and body?

Struggling on where to start? Why not do the thing that worked for me, and ask for God's help. Just three little words: 'Help me God.' And that is the start of your journey towards your experiencing healing in your heart. PS: Try to avoid the off-the-cuff 'heal me' prayers – try to dig deeper.

Enlightening Moment

Do you want to remain trapped or do you want to be free? You might think the answer is obvious but it is not. Make a decision today and let God do the rest.

Chapter Four

Pulling away from the crowds

remember reading a psalm of King David, in the Bible, and being thrilled to bits to hear him openly declare, as I have many times: 'Get me away from here!' Actually, those were not his exact words but that is what it would have sounded like today. Like me, David just wanted an escape from his troubles. His actual comments can be found in *Psalm 55:6-8 (MSG)* which states,

> 'Who *will give me wings,*' I ask – 'wings like a
> dove? Get me out of here on dove wings; I want some
> peace and quiet. I want a walk in the country, I want
> a cabin in the woods. I'm desperate for a change from
> rage and stormy weather.'

And if you read from verses 1–5, you will see how deeply overwhelmed he was by the challenges he was facing.

He wished he could flee to a secluded place for some tranquillity. And as he was no stranger to war and strife, one can only imagine that things must have been really bad for David to say this.

Now, if you will fast forward to our modern times, you will find that there are many who, like David, yearn to get away from difficult situations. I know, for sure, that I have experienced that yearning, and sometimes still do. Life can get so hectic and challenging at times that it can make us want to run for the hills and retreat for a while. Withdrawing from the crowd seems simple enough, but is there any harm in it?

Taking a retreat

Retreats, in themselves, are not bad. They can be a beneficial tool that can develop you as a person on many levels, spiritually and emotionally. By the way, notice I am using term 'retreat' as opposed to 'hiding'. Hiding is what Princess Leanne did and she was trapped for years. As for retreats, they are all about finding a quiet or secluded place to withdraw to. A retreat can be used for the purpose of prayer and reflection. By retreating, we are not stagnating: the purpose is to propel us forward; it is about personal growth, healing and restoration. Retreats provide the opportunity for us to be still in God's presence and draw closer to Him. In such an atmosphere, we can be comforted, nurtured, reaffirmed, healed and restored.

Over the years, I have truly come to appreciate the benefits of taking retreats. They have provided a setting where I could rest, look inside myself, address imbalances, catch up with myself, and identify and deal with unresolved issues prayerfully. Having done those things I am ready to re-emerge and put myself back into society. Retreats have been my haven where I could spend time with God, uninterrupted. There, I could simply 'be' and not have to 'do'. And taking a retreat has always been my first line of defence when facing perturbing, stressful, discouraging, or hurtful situations. Retreats are my refuge from the storms of life.

Eventually – and belatedly – I decided to take a retreat after my father passed away. I did the same a few years before that, after being involved in a major car accident. Both incidents traumatised me deeply, and I found that being able to withdraw from the crowds was a life-saver. It was not a luxury, as some people clearly thought. It was, quite simply, the thing that kept my head above the water – just about.

Since then, retreats (when done correctly, and not 'hiding') have become a necessity when I need to deal with certain situations I am facing. They enable me to move on and get back into the race. I treasure these moments. How soothing to my soul I find the experience – to be excused from the hustle and bustle of life, and allowed to be in the presence of My King.

I struggle, at times, to find the words to do justice to the benefits of my time alone. I can best describe the experience as a withdrawing from the crowds, as does a caterpillar when the time comes for its change into a cocoon. We too undergo a form of spiritual metamorphosis. And when the time is right, we re-emerge as a beautiful butterfly. When we consider the awesome benefits of taking a retreat, it makes us wonder why we do not retreat often enough or place a higher value on it.

God's perspective on retreating

Firstly, I would like to say that I do not believe God has an issue with us pulling away from the crowd. You only have to look at the life of Jesus Christ to see that there is a clear pattern of His retreating from the crowds. At times it was to pray, other times it was to rest or to enjoy fellowship with others. After a particularly busy time of ministry, we see Jesus suggest to the disciples they should go off by themselves to a quiet place where they can be alone (*Mark 6:31*). I believe taking time out at the appropriate times was His secret to His own success.

We also see Jesus giving us an invitation, when we find ourselves battered and bruised by life, in *Matthew 11:28-30 (MSG)*:

> *'Are you tired? Worn out? Burned out on religion? Come to me. Get away with me and you'll recover your life. I'll show you how to take a real rest. Walk with me and work with me – watch how I do it. Learn the unforced rhythms of grace. I won't lay anything heavy or ill-fitting on you. Keep company with me and you'll learn to live freely and lightly.'*

This invitation is about pulling away and coming aside to Him. With Jesus being our focus, retreating provides the platform where we can walk, watch and learn from Him on how deal with life.

God is all for us taking positive action to bring about balance and healing in our lives – and that includes our hearts. I believe this is part of His 'abundant life' strategy He desires for all of us (*John 10:10*). Moreover, from the beginning of time, He has given us charge over all things

– and this includes managing our own lives effectively and dealing with challenging and difficult situations.

From the time God sent Adam and Eve out of the Garden of Eden (*Genesis 3*), we see sin eating away at man's heart. Not long after their expulsion, we are told of the first murder, followed by all kinds of sin – so much so that it saddened God that He had ever created man. It is not surprising that we get caught in sin's crossfire. And, being fallible, we humans have a tendency to hurt one another and tread on each other's toes (at times intentionally). Being at the receiving end of all this can bring out the Princess Leanne in any of us. But you know what? Despite all of this, it is God's intention for us to experience victory over such situations. He does not want us to fall at the first hurdle. Seeing we have our life journey ahead of us, we have to do whatever it takes to rid ourselves of the harmful effects of life as they come at us. And retreats are a key to managing this.

When retreats go wrong

OK, the reality for some of us is that we have set up home in our castle permanently. Maybe you started out with the intention to take a retreat but you ended up hiding. You pulled away to find solace during a storm but the days have turned into weeks, the weeks have turned into months, and the months have turned into years. Moreover, the positive change, the healing and restoration, you were hoping for has still not taken place.

So how do you know your retreat has become ineffective? Here are some thoughts:

- You went on a retreat all right but here is what happened:
  - A raft of negative emotions, such as fear and lack of forgiveness, showed up and you were not able to move beyond this point.
  - You became consumed with self-pity and thoughts like, 'How could they possibly do that to me?', 'I cannot believe that happened', and 'But I thought they cared!'
  - You keep reliving the hurtful experience. It turns over and over in your mind.

Patricia

Patricia fell into this trap when she decided to take time out to deal with her bitter experience of being betrayed by a close friend. She thought she was doing the right thing, as someone in church had suggested this course of action. And it was, except that it did not work out the way she expected. All her pent up anger, hatred and bitterness rose to the surface as she kept reliving the experience. She cried, she wailed and she screamed when she remembered how her childhood friend, whom she thought had her best interests at heart, had started spreading false rumours about her having had an affair with one of the church elders. With her integrity and reputation in tatters, Patricia found it difficult to make eye-contact with anyone in church.

The idea of a retreat – away from the thick of it all – had seemed like the balm she needed. But Patricia was to find that she came back worse off than before.

- With no support in helping you deal with these difficult emotions, you return from the retreat in exactly the same place you were in before. (One point I would like to make, however, is that these feelings are always quite likely to show up at one's retreat – but it is what you do with them that really counts.)

• The retreating experience does not become an opportunity for growth and healing. Instead, you form the wrong kind of notions and conclusions:

- *Being a nice person gives you nothing but trouble.* So you will stop being nice. I wonder if Tamar blamed herself for being too kind, caring and obedient – positive attributes which nonetheless resulted in her rape. Had she disobeyed her father or been 'bad', would it have happened?

- *Being convinced that all people are bad.* After her 'wicked dragon moment', Princess Leanne incorrectly assumed that everyone was a danger to her. You may find that you have painted everyone with the same brush, and have come to a similar conclusion.

- You find yourself saying, 'I'll never let that happen to me again' or 'No one is ever going to hurt me like that'. On the surface, these seem like good mind-shifts to make, coupled with corresponding actions such as creating stronger personal boundaries, breaking off abusive, 'bad' relationships, and having a supportive network. All these things, as we know, can contribute to the healing process. Except when your mind-sets are driven by your negative experiences. And so, without working on this or adopting specific actions to move yourself forward, you remain stuck.

• You developed a number of defence mechanisms that you use to keep people away or avoid being hurt. Tamar hid herself away in her brother's house and Princess Leanne hid in her castle. Whilst you may not have not barricaded yourself in physically, you have found strategies to hide certain aspects of yourself (heart, feelings and emotions). The real issue still remains, and you continue living your life whilst carrying around emotional junk.

• Although you went on a retreat, you lacked the necessary knowledge on how to progress forward (akin to Princess Leanne losing her keys and not knowing how to unbolt the drawbridge). So you do not get the outcomes you desired – as Patricia found to her detriment. There is a quote from the Bible that says, 'My people are destroyed for lack of knowledge ...' (*Hosea 4:6, NKJ*). Ignorance is *not* bliss – and what you don't know *can* hurt you.

- You lacked specific goals and a plan of action, mistakenly thinking that the very act of withdrawing and doing nothing would do the trick. Wrong! Jesus always has a reason to withdraw, such as to rest and pray. I believe David also had a motive in *Psalm 55*. He was in search of peace and quietness, thinking – most probably – that a change of scenery would fuel a fresh hope, renewed strength and a new perspective. Getting away is the first step of the journey. But there is more to it – as Patricia came to discover.

- You did not make God the cornerstone of your withdrawal. Thinking you can recover after a life-challenging ordeal all by yourself, without God, is a futile activity. When I leave God out of the loop, it is like I am saying to His face, 'I got this one covered!' But, thinking I could hack it on my own – without the need for God – is a big mistake!

- You did not visualise, in your heart, that your retreat would have a positive outcome. And if you went there with negative feelings – continuing to apportion blame, rant, etc. – no change was ever going to happen. You need to prepare your heart and mind for the change you want to experience on this potentially life-changing journey. Unless you do so, you will retreat as a caterpillar and come back as one.

I am hoping you can now see how retreats and the act of withdrawing from others can go wrong. With that knowledge, you will understand how we need to take care so our efforts do not become futile, lest we remain trapped.

Journaling Moments

–When you have withdrawn from people, were you retreating for purpose to be restored or were you hiding? Only you know the answer to this. Search your heart.

– On reading this section, which points did you find yourself identifying with in regard to good and bad retreats?

Part 2

Letting the
drawbridge down

Chapter Five

Experiencing freedom from hurt

know, without a shadow of doubt, that freedom from hurtful life situations is possible. I write this book in testament to this fact. However, I believe that for healing and restoration to take place, you have to want it.

It is up to you to decide if you want to remain bitter or become better as a result of your life experiences. This is a choice no one else can make for you. And, once you decide to no longer live as a victim of your circumstances and be a 'victor', your healing experience can truly begin.

There were times when I struggled to make that decision. But I knew I had to move forward lest I became ensnared for the rest of my days. Why did I struggle? Because I felt that if I were to let go of my hurts, somehow I was belittling my experiences. And that wasn't all: I was uncomfortable relinquishing the power I felt that I had over the situation and those who hurt me. Being confronted with the suggestion that I should stop reliving the hurtful experiences, let go and forgive made me feel like another injustice had been done to me. Remaining 'hurt' gave me a false sense of power over the situation. Whilst it seemed no one else cared about my plight, I could keep the memories alive. That was the only power I felt that I had left. In all other respects, I felt powerless: I could not take the law into my own hands; I could not send legions of angels to hurt anyone who had hurt me; I could not force God to punish them. I could do nothing but keep the situation(s) in my heart.

The moment I felt anyone (God or others) confront me about my attitude at this time, it hurt even more. I thought, 'Do you know how much they hurt me? Can you even begin to understand the pain I went through? And now you are telling me to relinquish all that – to forgive and forget?' I got angry at people preaching to me: *How dare anyone tell me I had to let go of those who hurt me, without some form of justice.* For I had weighed up the crime in my heart and declared them guilty as charged. And that was that.

It took a while for me to move from a 'victim' mentality to one of 'victor'. But when I did, everything became so much better. I will be using the remaining chapters of this book to explain those strategies God taught me on how to move from that dark place where I was a prisoner into the place called freedom. This journey included opening up the doors of my heart again and learning how to love people once more. God taught me how to deal with my mindsets – learning to let go of the hurt, along with the perceived power I thought I had. Real power, I discovered, came about when I soared triumphantly over situations that could or should have crippled me. Power came by seeking an alternative life to hiding, living free of unhealthy emotional entanglements, and pursuing the abundant life.

And so, I chose real power.

And now, over to you!

Are you ready to let go of your hurts and pains? If not, you might as well put down the book and pick it up another time when you feel that you are ready. If you choose to let go, I congratulate you for making a decision that will change your life positively, forever. I hope and pray you gain the courage to deal with those difficult issues that have contributed to the woman we see today, so you can press beyond them and live the abundant life God has in store for you.

Inspiring Bible Quote

' "For I will restore health to you and heal you of your wounds," says the LORD …'

(Jeremiah 30:17, NKJ)

Enlightening Moment

Make the decision today to either...

- – Remain a victim or live as a victor

- – Be bogged down by your pain or experience the freedom of healing

- – Keep living in the past or look forward to a great future

The choice is yours!

Breaking free from your castle

Regardless of the hiding strategy you have adopted or the 'castle' you have fled to, your objective is to break free. Like with any prison break, you will need a plan – not only to get you out of the prison, but to keep you out for good. No more prison sentences for you from here on!

As you will have seen in movies of prisoners breaking free, it is never an easy task. Inmates do not just tell the prison bosses (who in your case might represent emotional baggage, strongholds, and forces resisting your freedom) to let them go. Nor do they simply say magical words like, 'Open sesame!' to the gates, whereupon – lo and behold – they swing open. It is a bit more complicated than that. As much as I would like to give you a security code to disable your drawbridge and make it swing open, I have no such thing. Nor can

I wave a special wand to bring you out of hiding, at the same time zapping away your unhealthy attitudes, beliefs and behaviours towards others.

I do, however, have an alternative – something that worked for me. When I set out on the journey I decided to get reinforcement: I brought God in on the situation. I was fighting a losing battle on my own; I could not navigate my way out of my hurts much less experience freedom from them. Here is what I needed to break free:

- I needed Someone who had a track record of healing troubled hearts and wounded souls.

- I needed Someone to stand in my defence when I was being accused of the part I played in the hurtful experience or my sometimes ungodly reactions.

- I needed Someone to carry me on certain days of my journey when my legs gave up and I could progress no more.

- I needed Someone to counsel me on the steps I must take to reach a place called 'freedom'.

- I needed Someone to shed light on my situation and reveal the truth to me – truth I sometimes could not see or chose not to see.

- I needed Someone to comfort me in my darkest days and reassure me that everything was going to be OK.

- I needed Someone who would be my constant companion – not just through this season but through all the seasons of my life.

I needed Someone who could provide unconditional love as a father, because there were times I was scared to bits, like little girl frightened of the dark.

'Why God?' you might ask. 'And not someone like a trusted friend?' Well, I weighed up all the attributes I was looking for and realised that 1) no one person on this earth has the capability I needed and 2) even if I found someone who had an iota of what I needed, I would be putting a tremendous pressure and huge expectation on them. The fact is, by themselves, they have not the power to heal. Whilst God may anoint someone to pray with me or lay hands on me, the fact remains that it is still God doing the healing.

Am I saying there is no need for the support of people on this journey? Absolutely not! So please, do not shut them out. After all, God may be answering your prayers and helping you through them. He often (if not always) uses people to accomplish His will. Whilst God <u>can</u> come down and give me a hug and wipe away my tears (the direct approach), He can also send people (known and unknown to me) to do the same (the indirect approach). And whether the approach is direct or indirect, the outcome is the same: I am comforted.

I came across a lovely Bible quote that exemplifies this idea, in *2 Corinthians 1:3–4 (AMP)*:

*'Blessed be the God and Father of our Lord Jesus
Christ, the Father of sympathy (pity and mercy)
and the God [Who is the Source] of every comfort
(consolation and encouragement), Who comforts
(consoles and encourages) us in every trouble
(calamity and affliction), so that we may also be
able to comfort (console and encourage) those who
are in any kind of trouble or distress, with the
comfort (consolation and encouragement) with
which we ourselves are comforted (consoled
and encouraged) by God.'*

So please do not be like the person drowning who was
calling on God to save them yet shunned the lifeguards
and passing boats who came to offer help. *He does work
in mysterious ways* ... Focus on only one avenue or
solution and it could be to your detriment.

Enlightening Moment

Now would be a good time to assess your
relationship with God. What is it like? Do you
believe in Him? It may be worth your thinking
about this.

Whether you are a Christian or not, God is
ready to step in and support you. You just have
to ask Him. If you are ready to do so, enlist His
help today and invite Him into your life.

Not sure how to? Say the following prayer ...

'Dear God, I invite you into my life and heart today. I ask that you forgive all the things I have done to hurt You and others. I accept that the Lord Jesus died on the Cross for me. And because of this, I now belong to the family of God. Help me on this journey I am about to take and free me from my painful life experiences that have caused me to hide from others. Thank you in advance for healing my wounded heart and troubled soul. In Jesus' name. Amen.'

Giving God access to your heart

I often wonder what the outcome would have been if Tamar had gone to her father, King David, and told him about what had happened. I reckon if she had done so, the ending to her story would have been different. I like to believe that, as David heard his daughter recount her ordeal, he would have reacted pretty much as would any father. Firstly, she would have received comfort and support and then, ultimately, restoration. Why? Because that is what fathers are meant to do. Secondly, being the king and a man of war, he would have acted in a way to bring about justice for the crime committed against her. As a result, whilst his actions might not have wiped away the memory of the heartbreaking event, Tamar's ending may have been somewhat different.

If we picture how a fair and loving earthly father might treat us, just imagine how much greater is the love and justice of our heavenly Father. We must not hesitate to run to our Father. He can give us much more than David would have been able to offer his daughter, Tamar, had she asked. Hiding from God is not the solution. It is about bringing our all to Him.

Going back to Tamar's story, I recognise that taking the bold step to approach her father would have been challenging for her. I have no doubt the 'word' would have spread around town. The journey to the palace alone would have been painful, had she made her way there in the royal carriage from her brother Absalem's house. What would the people have thought as she journeyed there? She might have endured stares, sniggers, insensitive comments, gossiping, accusations and blame. Someone might have shouted 'harlot'. After all, she had lost her prestige as a virgin princess. One can only guess how they saw her. But would they show her, the victim, any compassion at all?

If her troubles had happened today, she would, no doubt, have faced various camps: the finger-pointing 'you-should-have-known-better' accusatory mob; the 'get-over-it' crew; the 'you-no-longer-fit-in-with-us' lot; the 'let's-ignore-her' clique; the 'pretend-it-never-happened' group; and my absolute favourite: 'reassuring-by-mouth-but-nil-by-action' posse. Oh and let us not forget the media frenzy – the chat/reality shows, tabloid headlines, and social media posts that would make a killing from the scandal.

If there had been a well-meaning group that had wanted to reach out to her, their efforts would, most likely, have been hampered either by the other camps or their not knowing how to handle a high-profile rape in the family, temple or community.

Let us continue to imagine Tamar's situation. Her journey to King David's palace was not the half of it: once she was there she would have had to walk past servants (who were no more sympathetic to her plight that those who threw her out of Amnon's house after she was raped); she would have met men of the king's court (who might have terrified her, after her ordeal at the hands of another courtier – after all, if her brother showed no regard for her, why should they?); she would have to walk past her father's advisers who might have swayed his judgment of the case against her. The whole journey would have triggered post-traumatic flashbacks. She was already battling with depression, anxiety, nightmares, feeling emotionally numb, and the desire to avoid others. It must have been hell.

But do you know what? Your journey to your Father – God – does not have to be like that. Regardless of what you have been through and where you are on your journey, the great news is that you can approach God – hassle free – from the comfort of the chair on which you are sitting reading this book today. The good thing about your Father is that you do not need all the drama and trauma of making a physical journey to talk to Him. You can make that spiritual journey right where you are today. You no longer need to hide from others or fear their actions because you can have a private audience with your Father, the King, right here, right now. No need for shame, blame, guilt, feeling alone, or suffering in silence. You can pour out your heart to God today – risk free!

Journaling Moment

Are you willing to come out of hiding today and open up your heart to God about your ordeal – past or present?

Tell Him how challenging you found it all and how you have tried to cope. Tell Him how you felt your experiences no longer qualified you to carry the title of 'princess'. Tell Him how, like Tamar, you have tried to tear off your royal robes and put ashes in your hair so that you no longer resemble the precious woman and daughter He made you to be. Tell Him how you have tried to make it alone but that it has made no difference to your broken heart.

Now invite God into your situation. You do not even have to go and find Him. He is already there, next to you, with outstretched arms.

Enlightening Moment

God is ready whenever you are! He will make things happen. You do not have to worry about the what, where or how. All you need to focus on is allowing Him in.

Still not convinced you need God – much less grant Him access to your heart? Below are three reasons why you will need Him on this journey:

> **Reason one: you will need God's help** – As you make your way on your journey to wholeness, you will need the help of God to get you through it. Trust me, you cannot make it alone. So if you already know Him, simply invite Him along. And if you do not have a relationship with Him, there is no better time than now to start a relationship with Him. To do so, revisit the earlier prayer in this chapter.

> **Reason two: you will need to experience the love of God** – Without God's love, you will struggle to move beyond where you are right now. His love is redeeming, cleansing and healing. And by your embracing His love, you will also find it in your heart to release those who have hurt you, and build relationships with people (we will come to this later).

> **Reason three: you will need His forgiveness** – At some stage in this journey, you will need to repent of your actions (e.g. unwillingness to forgive, bitterness, resentment, hatred) in response to whatever others have done to you previously. Part of the Lord's prayer says, 'And forgive us our sins, as we have forgiven those who sin against us.' (*Matthew 6:12, NLT*). By forgiving others, you too can enjoy forgiveness.

So, before you go on, take some time to reflect on the above three points. I encourage you to start your journey on the right foot by getting your relationship with God right. Trust me, He is your greatest Ally and Advocate. You will need Him each step of the way.

Inspiring Biblical Quote

'God is a safe place to hide, ready to help when we need him.'

(Psalm 46: 1, MSG)

Chapter Six

Starting your personal journey

Guess what? In this chapter, you are going to get the opportunity to embark on your very own retreat – the first of many God-encounters. I am calling it a mini-retreat for the purpose of this book but feel free to adapt it to meet your specific needs. Please note we are not hiding here. In fact, hiding is no longer in our vocabulary as God's daughters. We are simply pulling away and giving ourselves the permission to pause so that we can uncover the hurt we have been carrying around with us.

In order to do this, you will need to prepare yourself. What we have covered so far in the book contributes towards your preparation. I will provide you with some guidelines about the retreat itself later, but you may find it useful revisiting the earlier chapter on pulling away.

Part of preparing yourself also requires preparing those around you. You may want to tell certain key people that you will be working on yourself. Tell them you are taking a personal journey of healing and growth (just in case all what we have covered so far proves to be too deep for them).

I will tell you this now: you may face opposition. In fact, it is most likely. I remember when I shared with someone that I needed to pull away for a short while, after some serious bumps on my journey, I was told that my actions were selfish. 'Selfish?!' I thought? If I broke my leg, no one would bat an eyelid if I needed to go to hospital. So why do the rules have to change when I experience a challenging setback or a broken or wounded heart?

There would have been a time when my old 'people-pleasing' self would have abandoned the idea of taking time out so as to remain in good stead with those in opposition. But thank God I ditched that baggage! Instead, my answer is: 'WHATEVER! See yah.' Why? Because I have come to recognise that when I am in the 'Princess Leanne' frame of mind (i.e. present body, absent heart), no one stands to experience the best of me (and I suspect that is the case for you too). In a state of hiding, while I may continue with my day-to-day activities, I know I cannot give my best. Instead, I am distracted by my bleeding heart and traumatised soul.

In Princess Leanne mode, our 'castles' become a type of accident and emergency unit except that there are no nurses, doctors or specialists to treat us. A mini-retreat is certainly in order, and now that we know the difference between hiding and retreating, we will be taking time to do this effectively.

Preparing for your retreat

After years of going on retreats, I have discovered certain strategies that have worked for me, which ensure my time is spent effectively. These guidelines keep me focused and stop me from gradually slipping into hiding mode. I encourage you to read through them and consider adopting them for your retreats. (By the way, please bear in mind that I will not be getting into detail about the different types of 'people-support' you can get – whether it is on your retreat or beyond. There is plenty of support out there, and my objective here is to provide you with some basics on which you can choose to build, however you see fit or are led by God.

Have a specific goal in mind

Without a specific goal or intention, your retreat could end up being a futile event. I am not saying you should have it all figured out before you go, but do have something in mind: an objective you want to use the time to accomplish. There have been times my heart yearns for respite though I cannot pinpoint why, and there seems no obvious reason for it. My objective then is to uncover, in the retreat, the reason for my restless unease, that feeling that I am carrying a burden.

At other times, the purpose is clear: tackle an unresolved issue, gain strength for a challenging season, pour out my thoughts and feelings to God, overcome a loss/ disappointment, be refreshed, etc. (Retreats can be used for all sorts of things.) Sometimes, I write my objective(s) in my journal, before I go, to serve as a reminder.

Journaling Moment

If you were to go on a retreat this moment, what would your goal(s) be? Could it be one of the following: to rest, reflect, refocus, be restored, healed, comforted, rejuvenated, refilled, reaffirmed?

Feel free to add your own personal objectives.

Make God the centre of all you do

One of your key strategies in retreating is making God the foundation of all you do. Before you even step out on your retreat, pray to Him that it might be successful and meet your goals. Use the retreat to (re)connect with God. Your dialogue with him should never stop, either on the retreat or afterwards. He is the One who will bring about the growth and healing you desire. You can connect with Him through prayer, reading His Words in the Bible, fasting, through songs, nature (I always feel closer to him and hear Him more clearly when I am by water, sitting under tree, on a hillside, etc.), and stillness with no distractions. And when you do this, you will discover that you start to bring Him into all aspects of your life on a day-to-day basis. This way, you no longer feel alone or isolated, regardless of where you are or what you face.

Prepare your mind

As you start to make plans for your retreat, I strongly encourage you to direct your mind towards the goal of making and experiencing positive changes in your life – even if it is only a small step but one in the right direction. Do not be blasé about it. Remember, it is your life, wellbeing and healing we are talking about. What you put into the exercise will determine what you get out of it. It matters not how expensive the venue was, how anointed the speaker, or hallowed the ground. It is what you put into it that counts. Prayer is the key, so pray about the retreat and pray for yourself that you will achieve your goals. Tell God what you would like to take place. For example, there are times I specifically want to hear God's voice, so I hold this thought in my mind.

There have been times I have gone on retreats recklessly without preparation, only to get there and find my mind is distracted with inconsequential things. I get so sidetracked that I cannot focus. Sometimes, too, things can go wrong that impact negatively on your experience. I attended one retreat, at a particularly busy time in my life, where I was so determined to have a great time but did not stop to take a moment to pray about it. I really needed the break. Being a group retreat, we had been told we would be assigned a room-mate upon arrival. I had not given this much thought, or prayer. Yes, I wanted to get on with the lady and I set my mind accordingly – but forgot to pray about it. When the time came, and I was paired up with a lady who talked non-stop, day and night, I found the experience almost intolerable. I went to bed with my iPod plugged into my ears with tears streaming down my face on the first night. The lady was perfectly nice, but I was crying out for some rest. It was only then that I thought to pray about it. Through the tears, I begged God to help. The following day, my room-mate came to apologise to me. She said that God had told her she was talking too much and needed to stop; if she did so, He said, she could learn something from me. My jaw almost hit the ground! From then on, I took preparation for my retreats more seriously.

Another aspect of preparing your mind is managing your expectations. God can use a retreat to change us instantly, but I have found that – more often than not – He chooses to use the retreat to set us on a journey. Just as Rome was not built in a day, it may be God's desire to take you by the hand and lead you step by step – because that is what He knows you can handle.

Journaling Moment

What preparations can you start to make before you embark on your retreat? What are your expectations for this journey?

Embarking upon your retreat

Now you have spent some time preparing your mind and spirit, the next steps is all about practicalities of the actual retreat.

Craft a retreat that works for you

This is important as it can have an impact on your outcome. You need to craft a retreat that works with what is going on in your life, and fits in with the time you have, and your budget. A retreat location can come in any form. It can be a retreat/prayer centre, conference venue, hotel, a friend's home, a park/beautiful grounds, etc. Pick one that works well for you, your resources (budget and time), and your goals. You may need to be creative to maximise those resources you have available to you.

There are times I would love to get away but, because of previous commitments, I have been unable to simply disappear. At these times my retreating space might have been the following: my bed (it has been a place of healing for me hundreds of times); my guest room (gives me a change of scene); my prayer space; a long car journey where I am driving solo (I cherish these times with God); a nearby lake (brings a sense of peace); my local steam bath/sauna (brilliant during off-peak times); my local library or coffee shop (my secret hideaway when I want to read or write); or a plane trip (thank God for window seats and headphones. In a few moments after take-off, it is just me, the sky, and God).

As for timing, there are no right or wrong answers. A retreat can be anything from a few hours, days, or even weeks. Experience has taught me that, rather than wait for the times I can go away for extended periods, I should maximise the moments I do have here and there. And so, every so often, I may take a weekend off at home to just be with God. You make do with what you have available to you. It really is about creating a space that is appropriate for you. And, that way, you do not have to wait till you have saved the money or holiday days. Use what you have got to get what you want. Do not let money or time become hindrances.

Journaling Moment

What ideas do you have on retreat locations currently accessible to you now? How much time and money do you have?

Plan a retreat to work through the ideas you have gleaned from this book. It could be a day, a weekend, or a series of dates.

Going solo versus going with a crowd

I believe this all depends on what you want to achieve. At times, I have found going by myself most useful because aspects of my job/calling very often require me to be in front of a crowd, whether it is speaking at a conference or giving seminars, being at an exhibition, or hooked in through social media. Like Jesus in *Mark 6:31*, the journey gets busy and I just want to pull away – whether it is, quite simply, to catch up with myself, or to hear myself think. There are also times when I feel God calling me aside for a one-on-one. If I have dragged someone else along on a retreat then this just does not work.

On the flip side, I have also come to value retreats organised by friends, groups, churches, or ministries. It is great when I do not have to be the organiser, or even the minister (i.e. work!). In these situations, someone else has paid the price for me (thankfully) and I can prepare my mind for what God may have in store. I have been on successful prayer retreats, with a friend or two, where we feel we are facing similar challenges and want to support the other. I have also been to retreats organised for the purpose of rest, healing and fellowship. These too have been excellent, especially those which are not too full-on and allow for some personal time of reflection (as I explained, I have introvert tendencies and need time to reflect and gather my thoughts). When room is not created for this, I do not seem to get the best out of the retreat. Balance is the key for me, as I am certain it will be for you. What sort of retreat you embark upon will be decided by your particular purpose for going on it.

Journaling Moment

What are your thoughts about going on retreats alone or with others? Which do you feel would work best for you? If you are unsure, plan to go on one by yourself as well as one with one or more individuals so that you can experience both types.

PS: If you have been a 'hider' and choose to go alone, do recheck your motives just to be sure.

Your retreat tool kit

What you need to take will depend on the type of retreat and its purpose, the venue, location, duration, and whether you go alone or with others. There some things that I feel are necessary for your journey in any kind of retreat: your Bible; a journal or recording device (depending on what works for you); music (this is not always provided at the venue and you will need to take headphones); and a book or two on the themes that fit with your purpose (a recorded teaching could also work). There will be other items that you will wish to bring – things that you feel will aid you on your journey.

* * *

These are strategies that have worked for me. I hope you find them helpful to you as you move away from hiding and start to embrace retreats as a tool to promote healing. Feel free to adapt them as you see fit, so that they work for you. As for your next step, you may, at this point, choose to continue reading the rest of the book or embark upon a retreat of some kind, and continue working through the book there.

Chapter Seven
Uncover your hurtful experiences

Now that we have set the scene for your retreat, the time has now come to start unravelling the truth behind your hiding. We have established that many of us use our hiding tendencies as a way of dealing with our wounded hearts and now my question to you is: what sent you hiding?

You may not be able to reel this off in a second. There are times we have been hurt and do not truly know how, by whom, or when. I would encourage you to contemplate prayerfully your response: ask God to give you an insight. And if you do think you already have the answer all figured out, I still encourage you to pray so that the Holy Spirit, the Spirit of Truth, can enlighten you still further.

While you are poised to get clarity on the issue, I ask that you be open to the many ways God might speak to you. He can reveal so much to you through all kinds of different means (e.g. movies, songs, books, dreams and visions). So, as I have cautioned before, do not get fixated on the heavens parting and your hearing a loud, booming voice – or an angel coming to visit (though they could both happen!).

Having God on board can also been useful when you want to uncover the underlying reasons for negative or strong reactions you might be feeling towards certain people, places or memories. These reactions can be a pointer: helping to trigger further exploration on your part. Ultimately, God's aim is to make you more self-aware. And you know what? Knowing brings with it accountability and a call for action.

To help you along, when you are finally settled in 'retreat mode', read through the rest of this chapter – making notes of what comes up for you.

Getting clearer

What actually happened (who, what, when, how)?

Natasha

Natasha had always felt overwhelmingly uncomfortable around family members on her father's side, especially when they had come to visit. It was something she had begun to notice more and more as she grew older, although she could not put her finger on why. And, even after leaving home and settling into her career after university, the sick-like feeling would come at the mention of certain names. With the 'feelings', she was having recurrent nightmares where she was being chased by two fierce-looking, faceless men. Sometimes she would wake up just before they hurt her. At other times, they kept pursuing her and showed up in places that she thought were safe.

Natasha decided to speak to one of her Christian friends, Bethany, who had trained as a counsellor. Through their conversations, prayers, and floods of tears, it came out that Natasha had been abused as a little girl, between the ages of three and seven, by two of her dad's brothers. It transpired that whenever her parents had needed a babysitter, they would often call on one of these two uncles. Her parents would also send her to their houses on weekends and school holidays as they seemed to enjoy having her so much.

Her parents could never understand why Natasha, who had been a happy baby, flew into fits of tears and uncharacteristic tantrums when they dropped her off. Or why, when they picked her up, she always looked forlorn and withdrawn. Yet still they thought nothing anything of it, even when she started to wet her bed – something she had never done before. They simply thought it was a phase, like her tantrums, that she would get over in time.

Happily for Natasha, when she was eight her father got a new job which meant moving away from 'the family'. Whilst Natasha was never subject to sexual abuse after this, the scars from her early childhood remained. She struggled with bed-wetting till she was well past her teens, and the nightmares persisted too. Moreover, she never seemed to be able to hold down a relationship, finding herself feeling sick and stressed at the point that the relationship started to become more intimate. At such times, Natasha would find a reason to call off the relationship.

Natasha has no doubt in her mind that if she hadn't opened up to Bethany, who counselled and prayed with her, starting the healing process, she would have remained in the dark despite being a woman of faith herself.

As you can see, Natasha had become a hider, and could never stomach (quite literally) intimate relationships with men for reasons unknown to her until she had the support of Bethany (and God) to help unravel her messy past. Prior to that, she was clueless as what had been causing her behaviour in relationships, nightmares, and physical symptoms.

Just like Natasha, I encourage you to seek dig deeper and get support of others, if necessary. Your goal here is to identify your hurtful experiences. By doing this, you can become clear as to the facts of the matter. Notice

I mentioned 'fact'. Your goal is to get to the truth. (Our hurts can also be related to our perceptions and feelings, which are heavily influenced by our life experiences, and may give us a skewed version of the truth.) There have certainly been times when I have become hurt and, as a consequence, developed a barrage of negative emotions towards an individual. Although I was quite certain I had perceived the truth of a situation, it turned out, in these cases, that my perceptions were inaccurate and I had let hurt settle in my heart over nothing. Your feelings can often be misleading, so do not always base your actions upon them. Our emotional reactions can be so powerful that they influence what we see, how we see, and, ultimately, how we respond.

We can look to the story of Princess Leanne to clarify this point:

- FACT: There was a wicked dragon who wanted to capture her

- FACT: She was traumatised by her wicked dragon incident

- PERCEPTION: The wicked dragon was still lurking the other side of the moat

- PERCEPTION: If she opened the door, the dragon would come in

- PERCEPTION: By hiding away in the castle, she would be better off

- PERCEPTION: Remaining behind bolted doors would somehow result in her recovery

- PERCEPTION: The dragon had tried to hurt her, thus other people might do the same

- PERCEPTION: No one cared about her

- PERCEPTION: Throwing herself into other tasks would take her mind off her experiences

So, while there were some truthful statements, the others were simply her perceptions – which were skewed by her experience of a previous trauma. If care is not taken, our whole lives can be consumed by the thoughts and perceptions that circle round our heads. We need to tease out the truth, and use it as a springboard to propel us forward. If we let one incident affect us this way, we can remain stuck forever – as Leanne did.

Journaling Moment

I have presented you with some thoughts around hurts that come as a result of *real* life experiences and our perceptions. So now take a moment to consider your life story to date. Have you amassed any hurts as a result of either? Think through each situation that may have put you in hiding and get to the root of the matter.

If necessary, enlist the help of a trusted other. Make sure that God is also in the centre of all you do.

Our wounds can be caused as a result of someone else being hurt (e.g. a dear friend, family member, or even someone you do not know). These I call 'third party wounds'. In such instances:

1. Your sympathy has turned into a barrage of negative emotions and unresolved issues towards the person who hurt the individual in question, although they did not hurt you directly.

2. As a result of this, you have responded as though you were the one who was hurt in the first place.

I am all for us bearing our brothers' burdens, but I do not believe this is the sort of burden God had in mind –

one that leaves you wounded too. Compassion yes, wounded no! It is one thing to feel a righteous indignation that might lead to reconciliation, justice, and healing for the involved parties, but it is quite another to let the situation eat *you* up inside.

Theresa

Theresa could only sit by and watch the way her father continued to ill-treat her mother – time after time. After all, she was only twelve. She could not fight him or speak up because that would have resulted in a flogging from hell. Where she came from, children don't answer back, much less tell their parents off. Not that it mattered anyway because the moment her dad had discovered she – their firstborn – was a girl and not a boy, his interest and involvement in her life pretty much ended.

So all she could do was watch as her father treated her mum like dirt. He never gave her mother any money to look after her and her five younger siblings. He sometimes took off for months on end, claiming he was on 'business', and never once feeling the need to call home or send any money. They all hated it when he came back because he was always shouting at them and calling them names. Her mother had been beaten a few times after questioning him as to his whereabouts, or arguing with him because of his late nights, drinking habits, and lack of care towards her and their children. Theresa dreaded the fights, especially after one of them had resulted in her mother being taken to hospital after the police were called. She is terrified that her father will find out that she dialled '999'. She believes, even now, that if he did, he would surely kill her.

From the tender age of twelve, Theresa settled in her mind that she would never, ever marry when she grew up.

How do you know if you have fallen into this trap?

- Gauge your reaction to someone who has deeply hurt one of your friends. Let us imagine that your best friend's ex-husband had physically abused her. What are your feelings towards him now?

- Have you made decisions and choices in your life as a result of someone else's hurtful experience? For example, using the scenario from the previous point, you have decided all men are evil, pretty much the way Theresa did at the age of twelve, and you will be having nothing to do with them.

What has happened here is that the ex-husband in question has become your 'wicked dragon', and now you have fled to your castle and are hiding from love. Can you think of any situations – which did not happen to you directly – which might have contributed to your barricading your heart?

Journaling Moment

Have you experienced third-party hurts? If so, what was the situation, how did you react and what was the consequence?

Lastly, let us not forget those wounds we may feel God has inflicted on us (or which He did not prevent), that have kept our hearts away from Him. Such wounds can be brought on by:

- What appears to be His lack of concern or love for us

- Our frustration regarding His slowness in answering our prayers or coming to our rescue

- Our anger and disappointment when He does not prevent certain situations from happening

And the list goes on ...

Delores

Everyone knew her as 'Sister Delores'. She was an active 79 year old who was always busy in her church – one she had been attending for over 75 years. It was there she had met her husband, Gerald, who had recently passed away, quite suddenly. Gerald had been her rock. If it hadn't been for him, she could not have coped with the death of their only child, David, who had been killed by a drunk driver a few days before his wedding to his childhood sweetheart.

With Gerald gone, she had no one to share her loss. When asked how she was coping, 'I'm fine, the joy of the Lord is my strength,' was her standard answer. After all, that is what she had been taught to say as a child. She was raised believing good and strong Christians never showed any sign of pain, hurt or discouragement (let alone talk about it) as this would have been seen as a form of weakness.

So, here she was, trying to 'be strong' and conceal her pain by keeping busy with church stuff. But, despite her efforts, when alone at home, the reality that her Gerald had gone forever hit her painfully. Gone were their daily walks along the beach, hand in hand. Gone were his loving arms around her and whispering of sweet nothings. Gone was her life companion.

And that is why Delores had struggled of late to pray. How could she pray to a God who would take away her Gerald? Why allow David – her only son – to die in the prime of his life? Did all her faithfulness and service to Him not count for anything? Why would He reward her this way?

Stuck with not knowing how to express her disappointment with God, Delores found herself drawing further and further away from Him.

Does all this sound familiar to you? Do not worry at this point about how you can move past these hurts. Your main concern, right now, is to gain clarity and self-awareness – empowered through God.

Journaling Moment

Have there been moments when you, like Delores, have felt hurt or disappointed by God? If so, how have you reacted to Him? What is the state of your relationship with Him now?

Now is as good a time as any to assess this and, if necessary, take steps to rebuild your relationship with Him. Remember, as mentioned before, you WILL need His support on this journey. So now is a good time to work on this.

Recognising patterns and themes

It is useful to know if your hurtful life experiences have come about as a result of:

1. A single major incident, something that might have occurred in childhood or adulthood.

2. An ongoing relationship or a pattern of relationships (e.g. where the same person keeps hurting you, or you keep finding yourself in similar unhealthy or hurtful relationships).

3. A series of unrelated incidents, both minor and major (e.g. betrayal of trusted friends, rejection, bullying, abuse, disappointment, or relationship breakdowns).

Tiffany

The whole of Tiffany's life, she had felt pushed around, that everyone was calling the shots. It had started with her adopted parents – who, in the name of wanting the best for her, had pushed her into taking ballet lessons and wearing dresses though she loathed them. And when it was time to make her career choice, they had done it for her, deciding that studying law was the best option and picking the University. Tiffany worked hard to please them and did well at University.

Then she landed her first job, and it seemed that her boss was determined to take up where her parents had left off, bossing her around and being overbearing. Never really knowing how to stand up for herself, she tolerated it. Day in, day out, her boss seemed intent on dictating how she should do her job.

If that had been all that Tiffany had had to contend with she could have coped, but since she had moved in with her boyfriend, James, a barrister who worked in the same high profile law firm, he just seemed on a mission to mould her into the perfect wife material. He picked out her clothes, told her how to wear her lovely long hair, how to behave with his upper/middle class friends, when they would get married, how the wedding was to be, how many children they were to have.

Despite noticing the pattern that had spanned pretty much her lifetime, Tiffany felt disempowered to do anything about it. How she wished she had the courage to stand up to them all, as opposed to resenting them and constantly crying about it.

Why is it important to pay attention to patterns and themes? As you have now embarked a journey to healing and personal growth, I believe it is useful to keep an eye out for these occurrences in your life. This can help you move forward in a number of ways, which might include:

1. Understanding your own patterns of behaviours and responses

2. Gaining clarity about your belief systems and the way you view yourself, others, and the future

3. Becoming aware of your vulnerabilities, strengths and personality styles

4. Discovering your thoughts and true feelings

5. Helping you put in place the right goals, strategies and actions

6. Aiding you in becoming more vigilant and spotting potential situations that may hurt you

They do say knowledge is power, and this new knowledge of yours will contribute to your healing and growth processes. It is worth mentioning that this exercise is not about apportioning blame to yourself or others. It is about finding out what drove you into the castle and kept you there, hiding from others. Along with greater self-awareness you will find those specific things you need to bring to God in prayer.

Journaling Moment

Can you recognise patterns and themes in your life? I encourage you to jot down what comes up for you.

Enlightening Moment

God knows what you have been through ...

> 'You've kept track of my every toss and
> turn through the sleepless nights,
> Each tear entered in your ledger,
> each ache written in your book.'
>
> (Psalm 56: 8, MSG)

Giving your cares to God

The bulk of this chapter has been about becoming aware of the life experiences that have got you to this point. 'So, now,' you ask, 'having uncovered all this stuff, what do I do now?'

Well, before we go to the next chapter, I want to leave you with something I hope you will find useful – as I do not want to leave you carrying what you have uncovered without support. What I would like you to do is hand it over to God.

I want you to picture the following:
'You are sitting in a waiting room, like at a doctor's surgery. Like you, there are many other women, dressed

in drab colours and looking rather sullen, waiting their turn to be called in. You notice that the women are carrying a bag, or luggage of some sort. Some have large rucksacks, others little handbags. A few have huge suitcases and trunks they can barely carry. Every so often, an attendant comes into the room and calls out the name of a woman, who gets up and carries her baggage with her to the room marked 'Healing Room'. When a woman struggles with her load, the assistant rushes to her aid, and carries it for her.

While this is going on, other women arrive – each carrying bags of varying sizes. They too, wait to be called in.

When a woman reappears from the healing room, you notice that she looks completely different. Her face beams with joy and her clothes are no longer drab-coloured but vibrant – to match her new countenance. Moreover, she no longer has any bags or luggage, and she is light on her feet when she skips out of the waiting room.

By now you are very curious as to what has been going on in the Healing Room. The weight of your own baggage, which is sitting on your lap, reminds you of your need to be healed. For your bag is filled with those hurts and pains you have collected in life, and your wounded heart bears the scars.

Then your name is called. You pick up your bag and are reminded, once again, of its weight. Seeing you struggle, the assistant is by your side in a second and offers to take your bag. He then leads you into the Healing Room. Upon entering, you immediately notice the light is so bright that it takes a moment to adjust your eyes to it. And when you look again, you see a man sitting at a table with a welcoming smile. He motions you to sit down and the assistant hands you your bag. As soon as you have done so, the man at the desk asks you to hand it to him, saying: 'Let me carry your burdens'.

It was as if the man knew what you had been carrying around. At first you are reluctant to hand the bag over, as doing so would mean he got to see all your hurts and pains. 'What will he think of me?' you wonder. But then you look down at the weighty bag and realise that it is too heavy for you to carry alone any more. 'What have I to lose by giving my burdens to him?' you think. 'After all, I have been carrying them all this while and have not been able to do anything about them.'

And so, you hand over the bag which the man places on the desk between you. He removes the tag from it, which had your name on it, and throws it in the bin. As for your bag, he hands it over to the assistant who takes it away to another room where all the collected baggage is stored.

The moment you release your burdens into the man's care, you feel a sense of relief. You are no longer burdened with the load you were carrying. For the first time in your life, you feel completely free. This makes you so happy that you start to smile. You thank the man and his assistant. The moment you step out into the waiting room, you notice that your drab clothing has become bright and colourful. As you walk past the waiting women, you cannot help humming a tune, as a feeling of joy has replaced the sadness and exhaustion you felt before. Baggage free, feeling like you are walking on air, you swing the door wide and take your first steps – as a woman who is now free from her hurts and pain.'

That woman is you. The man at the desk is God, your heavenly Father, and His assistant is Jesus. Together they take away all our baggage. Did you notice that you had to hand over your bag to God? He did not force you to do so, but asked you gently. Today, God is asking you gently to hand over your burdens and cares to Him, because He cares for you. Will you hand them over today? Your Healing Room is right here, where you are sitting.

If your answer is 'yes!', take a moment now, and hand over your burdens. Picture yourself as the woman in the Healing Room, approaching Him and passing over every pain, care, hurt and wound you can detect. Tell Him out loud:

'Father, I hand them over to You today, never to pick them up again. Help me live freely from my past hurts, that I have hidden from you and others. I choose to walk in your freedom, which you have made available through Jesus Christ. From today onwards, I am living the baggage-free life, in Jesus' name. Amen.'

Once you have handed over your baggage, picture yourself walking away, feeling light and relieved. Welcome to the new you!

Inspiring Biblical Quote

'Give all your worries and cares to God, for he cares about you.'

(1 Peter 5:7, NLT)

Chapter Eight

Forgive, and love again

A lesson on love

f anyone ever tells you forgiveness is easy, they are lying! It is no wonder that many of us struggle with it, especially when we weigh up the injustice on the scales of our minds and the person (or people) in question do not seem to deserve forgiveness. When facing such situations, in my frustration I would find myself asking Jesus just how He coped – dying for people, the majority of which did not give two monkeys about Him.

'How could you go to the Cross and die, when those you were dying for showed no remorse?' I asked Him.

I just did not get it. Surely, the person on the receiving end of the forgiveness should show some remorse? Or so I thought.

Questions like this ultimately got me pondering on the basis of my relationship with God. It was then that I realised, quite simply, that I had not gotten to grips with His love for me. Had I done so, I would not have expected harsh punishment when I myself sinned. He does not dish out punishment in the way our judicial system might. Although He does not condone sin, His love (and the work of the Cross) covers my multitude of sins. And when I receive grace and mercy, I do not need to figure out how to pay Him back. What an 'A-ha' moment this was for me!

At first, whenever Father would say He loved me, was proud of me, or was honoured by something I had done – as He often would – I had a hard time receiving His praise. I would fall to bits, crying, 'How could you?' – knowing, as I did, all those things I did or did not do. 'Why would you keep saying that?' I would often ask Him, thinking of those moments the next day when I was bound to have to repent of one thing or another. In response, all He had to say was, 'I love you, Gladys and that's that!' – and then more tears would flow. In fact the tears have not stopped, except that now they come for a different reason: that I fully grasp His unyielding love for me, regardless of everything I do!

Why did I mention all this? Believe me, it was not to make myself sound 'super- spiritual'. Instead, it was my way of explaining to you how God got me started on the path of forgiving others. His love for me never wavered, whether I read my Bible or not, prayed, or followed His laws to the letter. (Agreed, there are implications in not doing such things – the greatest being that I would fail to grow into the woman He desires me to be.)

The basis of all He does is love. As the Bible says, nothing can separate me from the love of God (*Romans 8:38*). And when I fall short of what He desires for me, I get on my knees and ask for forgiveness. And as I began to grow in Him, my love reciprocated, not wanting to offend Him. And so, through the demonstration of His love and forgiveness, I started to learn how to forgive and love others, in spite of what they did or did not do.

Inspiring Biblical Quote

'I'm telling you to love your enemies. Let them bring out the best in you, not the worst. When someone gives you a hard time, respond with the energies of prayer, for then you are working out of your true selves, your God-created selves ..."

Matthew 5:43–45, (MSG)

From love to forgiveness

And so, that is how God taught me about love, and followed it up with countless demonstrations of love, such as when He sends loving people my way. And, watching how He loves us, I started to see people differently – including those that hurt me. If God can love and forgive me as often as I needed, why should I have a different set of rules when dealing with others? His love compelled me to reciprocate.

No sooner had I had got to grips with this, than He started giving me opportunities to demonstrate those things I had learned. I guess you can say this was a holy set up. He would bring people's names to mind and I would ask, 'Father, how do I forgive someone who I know will hurt me again – as sure as there is a tomorrow?' And you know what His answer was? 'Just the same way I have to forgive you each day you sin.' I remember retorting, 'But you are God!' – as if to say that being God, He could take me hurting Him more than I could take others doing it to me.

I knew I was arguing a futile case and so I was forced to contemplate His answer:

'Just the same way I have to forgive you each day you sin.'

Wow, I had never seen it like that before! And I managed to see that, regardless of what anyone did to me or how often, I had to forgive them. I now see what Jesus was trying to communicate when He spoke about forgiving your brother seventy times seven times (*Matthew 18:21–22*).

It seemed a little harsh to me, because I had wanted to list all the grievances, all the pain they had caused me (as if God did not know!). But God instructs us to keep forgiving each other, no matter what. And it was the 'no matter what' that got me. I had compiled a list of the 'forgivable' and the 'unforgivable' but here God was, telling me to simply forgive. I had thought back over some of the hurtful life experiences, pretty much the same way you might be doing now, and thought, 'That's a hard thing to ask of me, Father.'

Recognising the inner struggle this was presenting, I asked God for help. I turned to the Bible and reminded myself of the life of Jesus. I then asked Jesus to give me a dollop of whatever He was 'on' that enabled Him to continue with His life's mission that culminated in His demonstrating ultimate love by dying on the Cross. Next, I enlisted the help of the Holy Spirit, my Comforter and Counsellor, to help me through what I knew would be 'dark' days – those times when the unrest deep within me stirred up, when one part of me would say, 'I have to forgive', while the other would kick back with, 'But you don't know what they did to me!'

I experienced such turmoil as I grieved over the hurt and pain I had stored up for years. It felt almost as if an appendage was being severed – like a part of me was missing. This, I now know, was a necessary pain that I had to endure in order to come out on the other side. But there was no getting out of it. If I claim to love as God loves, I must indeed forgive as He does – day in, day out.

A case for forgiving

Elizabeth (continued)

Elizabeth felt strange as she walked through the doors of her church for the first time in five years. She had struggled with the idea of attending church after her divorce with John. She could not bring herself to face her fellow parishioners after their scandalous marriage break-up. For both she and John had been respected in the church and there was talk of making them elders. And this had been, in part, the shame had kept her away.

But reconciling those feelings had not been the only motive behind her visit to church that day. She had been battling with high blood pressure for close to five years and had been on medication to manage it. Despite the medication, however, her health was not improving and she had been hospitalised on a few occasions as a result of related conditions. The high blood pressure had become a problem soon after the scandal had come to light. The state of her health did not surprise Elizabeth: after all, she had lived with a broken heart and a barrage of negative emotions for years. Her heart had been wounded by Johns various indiscretions over the span of her marriage. She had known what had been going on but had never confronted him or opened up to anyone else.

Having been overwhelmed by his betrayal and her own inability to forgive him, Elizabeth had boiled with anger, hatred, doubt and fear, but now the tears streamed down her face. The guest preacher that Sunday had started his sermon, and its theme: 'Forgive and love again'. It was clear the message was meant for her.

There are many 'Elizabeth-type' women – both in and out of church – who need to confront those past hurts that have kept them hiding, and ultimately trapped. Perhaps you can relate to Elizabeth's story. If so, the only way forward is to forgive all 'offending' parties – and that includes yourself, God and others. Part of Elizabeth's journey must include forgiving herself for not dealing with 'the pink elephant in the room' (her husbands affairs) when she got wind of them. Elizabeth, like many others before her, blamed herself for not taking a stand. The result having been an acrimonious divorce and a barrage of health issues.

Trickier still, is the notion of having to forgive God, especially when you feel let down by Him. How do you approach God to heal your pain when you feel He no longer warrants your trust? This is, perhaps, our greatest challenge, but one that is not impossible to overcome. It all starts with taking the first step, as Elizabeth did, to rebuilding your relationship with God.

Journaling Moment

Is there a lack of forgiveness in your heart towards yourself, God, or others? Now is a great time to pause and reflect upon the contents of your heart.

Now, over to you

In her book, *Extending the Olive Branch: Forgiveness as Healing*, Sharon Platt-McDonald mentions that medical research is now suggesting that we can learn to forgive in a way that preserves health and prevents disease – pretty much the same way we can learn to incorporate exercise and a healthier lifestyle to promote our wellbeing. Sharon goes on to share about the work of Dr Dick Tibet and his scientific study known as *Forgive to Live*. Through his research, his data demonstrates scientific proof of the health link between an individual taking a forgiveness training programme and the resulting significant reduction in blood pressure.

Through his book, *Forgive to Live – How Forgiveness Can Save Your Life* (ISBN: 978-1591454700), Dr Dick Tibet aims to help the reader reduce their anger and drastically improve their health – so they can move forward, no matter how deep the hurt. He believes that every one of us has what he refers to as 'a grievance story' – where we have all been hurt or rejected by someone who mattered to us. He reckons that, all too often, it has led to negative emotions – such as anger – that linger for years. As a result, Dr Tibet is convinced that forgiveness can literally save our lives and encourages us to follow this path rather than have our anger destroy us – spiritually, emotionally, relationally and physically (as we have seen happen, over time, in the life of Elizabeth).

I have to say that the link between forgiveness and our health does not surprise me. I guess God knows what He is doing when He continues to implore us, through His Word, to forgive. It is not that He is a spoil-sport or an unfair God. Way before the scientific community caught on, He knew full well the implications a lack of forgiveness could have on us – spirit, soul and body.

And now … over to you!

But you might be thinking, 'Do you know what they did to me?'. Perhaps tears welled up in your eyes as certain memories flooded back. If you have had to face harsh physical or emotional scars each day, as a result of your ordeal, you must wonder how anyone could expect you to forgive – much less love – the person, or people, who hurt you. I fully understand where you are at.

But you know what? God is loving and gracious. He understands *all* our earthly difficulties. He feels the aches of our hearts. He understands the pain we experience when our hearts get broken, when we are rejected, or treated badly or unfairly. Yet, He also knows the negative and damaging effects that being unforgiving can have on our spirits, souls and bodies. He knows that we, the hurt ones, are liable to end up captives of our own experiences – while those who hurt us go free. We are the ones who get trapped, stuck, and hidden away from others. And because He loves us too much to leave us in this state, He starts the healing work in our hearts – as soon as we allow Him in.

'How can I let Him in?' you ask

Just enter the healing room and hand over your baggage. Let down the drawbridge to your hideaway so that God can come into your heart and heal you. He is waiting to be allowed inside.

Something I learned a long time ago is that I cannot walk this particular journey alone. I cannot heal myself. And I cannot even begin to start forgiving others without God's help. It is just too much … more than I can bear.

So, knowing that, I did the smart thing and enlisted His guidance (no room for heroics here!).

And, yes, the journey to forgiveness can be hard. Some folk seem to think it is as simple as pressing a button on your forehead, labelled 'forgive'. Then – hey presto! – the deed is done. What they do not realise is that by jumping the various steps they need to pass through on the road to forgiveness – in going for the 'quick fix' – they find that real forgiveness is not achieved, and the good feelings they experienced for a time were not long-lasting.

I believe God processes us, one step at a time. He directs our steps in His ways (*Psalm 37:23*). As long as we are willing, He will dictate to our hearts what the first step is, on the ladder of forgiveness, and when to take it. Once we are there, our hearts will be given instructions to help us get on the next step, then the next – until you wake up one morning and think, 'I'm free!'

I encourage you to open your heart and listen for God's instructions on how to deal with your specific situation. Of course, He may use other tools to speak (as mentioned earlier) so keep your ears tuned in. How to remain tuned in? Let Him in and then remain close to Him through prayer, studying of His Word, and being around others who can buoy you up. Whenever I am in this mode, I have my spiritual antennae on. They invariably detect the potential helpfulness of someone who might come my way, or a book I come across. I quietly ask God to speak to me through the person or object. That way, if there is something I am not quite sure about, He finds a way to guide and inform me.

I remember one time when an incident happened between myself and a particular person. I was angry at them at first but then brushed it to the back of my mind. There, thankfully, it was not destined to remain as I had granted God access to my heart. One day, I felt Him do a 'spiritual spring clean' on me, which brought the matter back to the fore. I realised, when He did so, that I *still* had an issue with the person and that I was hiding. (I had withdrawn from them – no calls, nothing!) Just the mention of their name touched something sensitive inside me, and I had to admit that the issue was as present as ever.

Over the next few days, I started to pray and mull the issue over in my mind. I knew God had said I should forgive the person but it was easier said than done. I found myself stuck on the matter until something happened which caused a shift: a friend from abroad sent me an email. At the end of it, she mentioned the person I had an issue with by name, and said that she felt God wanted me to release the person from my heart. In a later email, she went on to share her personal challenges with forgiveness but described the freedom she had felt after she had taken the bold step. It was at that point that I turned to God, saying, 'What would You have me do?' Then, and only then, did I get the instructions I needed, and I faithfully obeyed. Today, the relationship has been restored. Are we best friends? No, but there is no longer any resentment in my heart. Moreover, I can pick up the phone and speak to them freely, as if nothing had happened.

God knows it is a struggle for us but, with a willing heart, anything is possible. All you need to do is be willing to follow His lead, be proactive, and take the steps to forgiveness. He may lead you to a certain scripture or book. He may instruct you to pray for those who hurt you, apologise to them for your reaction towards them, or even give the person – who has been a lifetime 'pain-in-the-you-know-where' – a gift. And you will find that doing such things does something to your heart. It unlocks the door to forgiveness.

Do not worry – you will not have to rely on your strength alone. If you keep praying to God, seeing Jesus as your Mentor, and enlisting the help of the Holy Spirit – as I did – you will get there. This, I found, was the way to make forgiving and loving others a permanent feature of my life. And trust me, there will be days when you feel overwhelmed and find you do not have the strength to go on. When you do feel helpless in this way, God gets stuck in. Compassionate and practical, He rolls up His sleeves and carries you on those parts of the journey you find hardest. (PS: He is *always* by your side!)

With God, all things are possible (*Luke 1:37*).

Enlightening Moment

Struggling with forgiving others? Declare to yourself, 'For I can do everything through Christ, who gives me strength.' (*Philippians 4:13, NLT*)". Grab Jesus' Hands and ask Him to walk the journey of forgiveness with you. Embarking upon the journey by yourself is somewhat futile. But walking with Jesus each day, step by step, is the only way! And, in time, the shackles of your lack of forgiveness will be broken.

Inspiring Biblical Quote

'At that point Peter got up the nerve to ask,
"Master, how many times do I forgive a
brother or sister who hurts me? Seven?"
Jesus replied, "Seven! Hardly. Try seventy
times seven.'

(Matthew 18:21–22, MSG)

Chapter Nine

Unlock your heart and install gates!

n the last chapter we learned about taking the first steps to forgiving others. The next step in this journey is all about unbolting the doors to our hearts, and moving away from our hiding tendencies in a safe and healthy manner. Part of this process will include learning to trust others, build relationships, and allow people into our lives. If the thought of this sounds daunting, do not let it worry you. This chapter will provide you with some ideas to help you along.

Allowing people access to your heart

Before we progress on this matter, there is one thing I need to say:

I am all for unlocking the doors to our hearts, but you cannot simply let anyone in!

Yolanda

Yolanda was blinded by love – literally. Years before, the final piece of physical abuse she had suffered at the hands of her ex-boyfriend Leon – which had sent her to hospital, yet again – had been different from the others that had gone before. Before, she would come home with cuts and bruises. One time she had suffered broken ribs; another a fractured wrist as she had tried to defend herself when he had taken a metal baseball bat to her.

But nothing could have prepared her for the news that final time. Her doctor had told her that her left eye had suffered irreparable damage. She would never see through it again. The cause of their fight had been the news that she was pregnant and had decided to leave him after the years of domestic violence. The news had sent Leon into a violent rage. All she could remember of the ordeal was his constant rant, 'if I can't have you, no one else will!' in between the blows that he had rained on her with his fist and bat. In hospital, the doctor had broken the other piece of devastating news: she had lost the baby, and in the attempt to stop the bleeding and save her life, they had had to perform an impromptu hysterectomy.

So, at the age of 25, all Yolanda had to show for her tumultuous and abusive eight-year relationship was a blinded eye and the fact that she would never, ever conceive a child again. Leon had certainly done his best to make sure that no one would want to be with her. Nothing would recompense her for the pain she had suffered, even his having been sent to prison. And she still could not rest: she had had to flee her town because he had sent word that he would finish the job once he got out.

Through a charitable Christian women's organisation, Yolanda had been relocated to a small village 350 miles away. It had taken years to get used to her new life. With counselling and the encouragement of her friends, family and the small village church she had started to attend, she could see her world coming back to some semblance of normality. She was gradually dealing with her pain. The women's group had been kind to her and she had received all the pastoral care she needed from the church. All of this had helped her finally to forgive Leon. She had felt able to go back to college (something Leon was always dead set against) and was now halfway through her social worker qualifications. After her ordeal, she was determined to help others avoid what she had gone through. In short, her future was looking brighter.

So you can imagine the shock she got when Leon showed up at the door one day, claiming to have become a Christian in prison, and now a changed man. He went on to tell her he was sorry for the hurt he caused and asked if she would take him back.

Yolanda did notice something different about him for a moment, but flashbacks of the worst night of life made her do one thing – slam the door shut!

I think a word of caution is necessary here. Yes, we do need to forgive and love others: as Gods children, we are compelled to do so. However, in doing so you should not let harmful people (back) into your life. And, anyway, it is impossible for you to be close chums with absolutely everyone. Rather, your ultimate goal is to be cordial to others, do your best to be at peace with people, and forgive as often as is necessary.

Below are two categories of people I suggest you be cautious about:

Category one: those who have hurt you in the past

God can change people's hearts, as I believe He is doing to yours through this book. However, it is important to realise that people are on different journeys, and that not all of us reach that place or, at least, not at the same time. So it would be unwise, and even unfair, to expect others to be where we are on the journey. I always say 'all fingers are not equal' to describe how we are all at various stages in the production line of God's factory. Proverbially speaking, you may be at stage five, out of ten possible stages, on the ladder to growth and healing, while another person may not have even yielded themselves yet to the 'processing' – let alone embarked upon their own processing journey. I suspect this is the case for Yolanda and Leon. Bearing this in mind, we need to give room for this.

When I come into contact with people, I recognise that they have their own story too – and perhaps have baggage of their own. It is their story that has made them into who they are today, the person we see. If we bear this in mind when we are dealing with people, we are able to step back and consider the bigger picture. That way, perhaps, we might see things as God might see them, rather than looking through tinted lenses. Doing this will promote compassion and forgiveness. Moreover, we can make more informed choices and decisions for our lives.

Hence, I think it is wise to be cautious when dealing with, or forming close relationships with, those who have hurt you, especially when their current behaviour patterns indicate no evidence of a changed heart. Let us say, for example, that you were in an abusive relationship with your ex-partner. You broke off the relationship and have spent months trying to overcome the effects of it – through your faith, counselling, prayers, and even relocating – pretty much in the way Yolanda did. In short, you have moved on, and you are getting God's help and the help of others to heal you. Then Mr Not-So-Nice-Man shows up professing his undying love for you. Do you let him in? While one small part of you might feel swayed by his protestations, you see that he has had no support to overcome his emotional/mental challenges and he shows no remorse for what he did. Then, when you try to explain to him that you have moved on, his old aggressive tendencies flare up, a sure sign that things have definitely not changed.

(I used an abusive ex-partner scenario here but this can apply to any emotionally-damaging relationship or hurtful experience.)

Can you see why you should be cautious? If there does not seem to be any change in that person, they may end up hurting you again. And, while you cannot completely avoid hurtful experiences or resort to hiding permanently, you can adopt healthy strategies to protect yourself.

Want to know what the future would be like if you let such a person back into your heart? Look at their past behaviours. Yes, you have forgiven them and you no longer hate their guts. But the fact that you have released them from your heart and chosen to love them with the love of God (even the Bible says love your enemies – *Matthew 5:44*) does not mean that you are compelled to prove it by going back into a relationship with them!

The same applies to all kinds of relationships. Imagine if you had been business partners with someone who had turned out to be a swindler, so that you ended up losing all you had. Again, the 'forgive and love' rule applies – but would it be wise to embark upon another business venture with them? I think not, especially as they have not demonstrated any new traits to show that they are trustworthy.

You may find that some people (including those who have hurt you) may try to manipulate you, encouraging you to think that by forgiving and releasing them from your heart you should pick up from where you had left off. Whenever that has happened to me in the past, I have reminded myself that I have nothing to prove to them. My allegiance is to my heavenly Father who wants me to live an abundant life, baggage-free. So, I listen out for His views on each matter. With His help, I can continually search my heart, and expunge clutter from it – *and* keep it that way.

Remember, we have a God-given right to protect ourselves and guard our hearts from people who are either out to hurt others intentionally (they do exist) or those who hurt others as a result of being hurt themselves. (Some might argue these two types of people are one and the same.) I suggest you give them room to be healed, restored, so that they might experience the life transformation you have yourself sought, through Christ.

It may also be that you are the one trying to re-establish a relationship to prove to yourself (and others) that you are 'over it', are stronger, and can handle it. If this is the way you feel, I would suggest you tread carefully and wisely, and ask yourself why you are feeling this way. Get some godly counselling from a trusted friend, family member, or someone who you know, out of love for you, would speak the truth, even if it is not what you want to hear. Be open and honest and tell them how you feel. Pray about the situation and see what God is saying on the matter. Does He want you to have a full-blown relationship, going back to the way things were, or for you to settle for being on speaking/neutral terms? Does God want you to break the relationship off (even if it is only temporarily, so that He has time to finish His work in you, and possibly in the other person)?

What is key to remember here is that God is concerned about the state of your heart.

There have been times when a person is utterly convinced that God wants them to rekindle their relationship with another. If that is where you are at (and with prayer and wise counsel you are convinced that it is right to do so), ask God for guidance on how to progress, and what changes might need to be made this time round. Wisdom really is key here – and you had better watch out for your emotions and previous experiences clouding your better judgement. They have a tendency to show up when you are least expecting it.

Category two: those to whom your instinct raises a red flag

Sade

From the moment Sade had arrived at her meeting with David and his business partner, Richard, something did not sit right with her. She hadn't been able to shrug the feeling off throughout the meeting. David and Richard had a business venture abroad and were looking to get new investors onboard. They had given a great presentation of their proposal and, on paper, the deal looked sound, promising a strong return. It had seemed to be one of those once-in-a-lifetime kind of investments.

Yet, Sade had had her reservations. David and Richard had done all they could to get her to sign on the dotted line and issue them with a cheque – as had been agreed – but she had decided to go with her gut, and said she needed to take some time to think about it.

After she left, the feeling had grown stronger and stronger. She just knew intuitively that she needed to be cautious and wait. Whilst she was a shrewd business woman and had made loads of money through such investments before, this one felt different. So, she had put the matter to the back of her mind. Then, a few weeks later, she heard that David's and Richard's company had gone bust. Had she signed on the dotted line, she would have lost a cool £100,000 – just like that.

The moral of the story? If in doubt, listen to your intuition – do not just brush these feelings aside and dive right in. Instead, you should pause – especially when you can't put your finger on what is bothering you, and yet you know that something does not feel right, as it was with Sade.

Take time out to reflect prayerfully on the situation – it could be God's way of trying to caution you. There have been times when I have met people and have felt instinctively that the relationship will not, and should not, be close. Sometimes God has showed me the contents of someone's heart – their intentions – through a dream.

And then at other times I have felt the need to pause when my head says one thing but my heart says another. And when I wait, God reveals stuff.

It is not like a person will have a devil's horns and tail – but the unease inside you cannot be shrugged off. And it may not even be that they are a bad person – it is just that the relationship is not right for you now, or maybe ever. At such times, I pause just to get some perspective:

- Might I be trying to overcompensate for my previous hiding tendencies?

- Can I see what God sees? (He always sees the bigger picture.)

God always sees the bigger picture, and it may not be one which you are privy to. But the great thing about remaining close to God is that He does reveal a piece or two of the jigsaw puzzle. By waiting and active listening, we get direction on what to do next. So, at such times, while I may not have actually cut off the relationship (unless I had felt led to do so), I cautiously hold back.

Please listen to the still inner voice in you.

PS: And watch out that your previous 'hiding' tendencies do not cast everyone in the role of 'wicked dragon' – even if they are perfectly harmless – or you will send yourself fleeing into your castle.

Guarding your heart

Guarding your heart is your responsibility, and I suggest you have some rules in place to ensure this happens. One simple one to start with:

Everyone cannot be and *should not* be in a deep and personal relationship with you.

Helen

Helen learned the hard way that not everyone can be trusted. When she had told Michelle and Tracey – two girls she worked with in the office – about her recent problems with her husband, how should she have known that what she told them, in confidence, would quickly spread like wildfire through the office. Even people on other floors got to know that her husband was cheating on her. One lady even came up to her and said she would not stand for it, if it were her.

Helen regretted pouring out her heart and wished she could stop the gossiping but it was too late.

The truth of the matter is, you cannot go around baring your soul to everyone, or giving your heart to all and sundry. Not everyone is mature enough to handle that; it would be akin to you 'casting your pearls before swine'.

Over the years, I have learned to take my cues from Jesus Christ. He had twelve disciples, and the three closest to Him were Peter, James and John. I noticed that on a few occasions when intimacy was required, He called on the trusted three. In the Garden of Gethsemane, it was those three that He took aside, to reveal the state of His soul and ask for their prayers (*Mark 14:32–42*). I often wondered about Jesus' approach: could the other disciples not handle seeing Jesus like that? Would it have affected how they saw Him? Were their hearts (which were not as closely knitted to Jesus as the others') still immature or unbelieving? Would having all the disciples there have caused other problems, such as arguing? I do not know what the answer is, but Jesus decided it was to the three He needed to unburden himself.

I too have been led to adopt this approach, enlisting help from a trusted few. I have learned to do this after having, in the past, poured out my heart to people that, in hindsight, I realised that I should not have. It was not that they were not well-meaning, it was simply that they were the wrong ones to speak to in those circumstances. There have been times when I have opened up to someone only to come away from the conversation having wondered why I had ever dreamed of doing so – they had been completely unhelpful, unsupportive, and lacking in compassion. At such times, I found myself running in the direction of my castle. There I created an unhelpful rule: 'Don't pour your heart to anyone. It's a waste of time.'

Happily for me, God helped me ditch that rule by helping me become more astute in building close relationships and linking me up with the right folk. It is great to have a wide network of people around us from all spheres of life, but we need to remember that they are not all close friends. Social media does not help the confusion. It can give users a false sense of friendship, the impression that because there are many people on our 'lists' that they are close friends. Whilst friendships may evolve through social media, the fact remains that a list of 'friends' might comprise business associates, acquaintances, former colleagues or friends, and others who are interested in you for a wide number of reasons. And you will save yourself a lot of hurt and pain by recognising this fact.

The other thing I have learned not to take too personally is when friendships grow apart. They can be seasonal: some people close today but gone tomorrow; others last a lifetime. But if you have found yourself extending a hand of friendship which is not taken up, try not to take the rejection too much to heart. Instead you need to guard your heart against the pain that can ensue from separation or rejection, because it can send us heading for our castles.

Something else I have learned is not to hang on to relationships when I should not (e.g. when driven by my own insecurities). I know doing so impacts my growth in this current season of my life. Instead, it is about knowing when my season is changing and how to change with it so I do not become stuck. Think of a tree moving into autumn but wanting to hold on to its leaves, despite the fact they have turned brown. They have to fall off to make room for the winter, before the spring brings new leaves.

Whichever way you look at it, your relationships will go through their seasons – their peaks and troughs – because, quite frankly, that is life. And prepare yourself:

this does include your close relationships, which may experience some form of testing. Your goal is simply be aware of this and to guard your heart against not only the action of others but your attitude and emotional responses to their behaviours.

Inspiring Biblical Quote

'Guard your heart above all else, for it determines the course of your life.'

(Proverbs 4:23, NLT)

Lastly, always keep in tune with your inner voice. By this, I refer to the Holy Spirit. He will guide you into all truth. And when you are unsure about anyone or what your instincts are saying to you, pause. Neither dive in, nor flee. Instead, get to the bottom of the niggling feeling and ask yourself:

- Is it fear-based? (i.e. the return of your old gremlins – the fear of potential wicked dragons.)

- Do you need to be cautious and check things out before you dive head first into a relationship?

- Is the person pushing for a close, intimate and trusting relationship more quickly than is normal for a relationship to progress? Maybe they want you to commit to the relationship (business or personal) which does not sit right with you?

- Is the person dragging their heels – maybe they are the one with their guard up. It does not make you an unworthy person; it is just that it was not meant to be.

Have you picked up verbal, visual and/or behavioural cues that show up a red flag? This is particularly important if you have been in an unhealthy or hurtful relationship in the past. If you see traits in this person that you feel you cannot handle, do not want to handle, or that you feel might be detrimental to you, please feel free to use your gates and lock them, keeping the other person the other side.

Put boundaries in place

OK, so now that God has started working on your heart, your next step on this transformational journey will be to put strong boundaries in place. This may seem daunting at first (especially if you have been 'away' for a while) but it is the right thing to do when you start taking steps (even baby ones) in the right direction.

The reality is that there are loads of wonderful people out there. The world is full of people who can love, encourage, support, and have fun with you – and to whom you can offer the same. God has people waiting in the wings to demonstrate His love for you.

And now that you are opening the door to your heart, you need to have the means to keep anything that is unwanted out. Just as you have a lock on your front door which ensures that you can allow friends and family in and keep burglars out, you will need gates to keep your heart safe. You would not leave your front door open all night or leave it unlocked when you go out; you will need to do the same for your heart.

There are some people in our world who would like to gain access to your heart for the wrong reasons. It is a sad fact of life, but one that we need to understand. Some of them are hurting themselves, but who are, in turn, driven to hurt others. There are others who take advantage of those they feel they can manipulate in order to get what they want. And, in rarer cases, there are those wolves in sheep clothing who are out to steal, kill and destroy. These people are, thankfully, in a minority but if they are seeking some sort of relationship with you it is unlikely that their motives are healthy.

So wise up, install your gates, and use them wisely. That way, you decide who comes in *and* who needs to leave.

Setting healthy boundaries

I have a further suggestion: that you have 'soldiers' at your gates. In simple terms, your soldiers represent your personal boundaries. These boundaries let people know what is or is not acceptable to you, along with possible consequences. For example, some women hiding from others do so as a result of others abusing their time, money, efforts, belongings, and even body. This might be an overbearing parent, family or friends who see you as their personal cashpoint machine, or a boyfriend who sees his girlfriend's body only as a means to satisfy his needs. When healthy boundaries are not in place, these relationships continue to harm us because we have not taken adequate steps to deal with them.

You may want to formulate your own list of boundaries, depending on your particular experiences, stating what is acceptable (or not). Here, to help you, are some scenarios where boundaries are needed:

- **An overbearing church leader** who keeps taking your time and money, while not seeming to care about 'you' the person. To this person, you are no more than a workhorse – all in the name of 'supporting the ministry'. In this case it might be a good idea to have a word with the person, explaining how you feel, rather than leaving the church resentfully, determined never to go back or help others again. (In short, going into hiding.)

- **A sister that takes you for granted** – who thinks that, just because you are single, you have no life of your own. And so you find yourself being lumbered with her five children, all under the age of eleven, several times a week – so that she can get on with her life. Again, you will need to stand up for yourself instead of letting it eat away at your heart and drive a wedge in your relationship. If you do not speak to her about it, you will find yourself avoiding her calls, and getting bitter and twisted inside. Come to an agreement that works for you, such as your having your nieces and nephews over for a few hours once every couple of weeks. Tell her that she can no longer show up at your door and expect you to drop everything.

(Better still, invest in your own relationships. Just because your sister is taking liberties does not mean that everyone else is like that.)

- **A friend who thinks you are made of money.** Recently, you seem to be doling out more cash to her than for your own personal needs. Each time she comes to you, the sob story gets worse: she was laid off from work; she lost her purse; the bank was closed; she needed to pay her electric bill. By now, you are feeling the pinch – and cannot remember the last time you had your hair done or went out for a meal. You know she is taking liberties but she always manages to make you feel guilty by pulling the 'Christian card' on you – as if it is your duty to take care of her needs. And so, as the resentment builds within you it starts to affect other aspects of your life. Anytime the subject of money comes up, even if it is about a charity or church fundraising effort, you flinch – and you stop giving to any cause. You have been hurt and now you have clammed up. The solution? Tell your friend straight up that your 'fund-a-friend' lifestyle ends today. Give her the option to carry on being a friend, and if she cannot live with this, feel free to show her the gates and lock them behind her. At least now you know what the basis was for your relationship.

- A boyfriend who decides to break off your relationship 'after all you have done for him'. You feel rejected and hurt, and immediately – in a kneejerk reaction – embrace the victim's mindset. But, whatever you do, do not hang up your 'love boots' and decide love don't live here anymore. You may never get to the reason why he broke the relationship off, but don't wallow over spilt milk. Learn the lessons you need to take from the experience and move on. (By the way, regarding your 'after all I have done for him' statement, do you need to think about what boundaries were, or were not, in place? What *did* you do for him? Was he doing all the taking, you all the giving?) Whatever you do, do not let this rogue experience deprive you of experiencing love, one of the best feelings in the world. Set boundaries before the next guy comes along.

You will notice from these scenarios that you are encouraged to heal the wounds by getting out there, being proactive, and confronting the underlying issue. In no case, is there a license to hide or accumulate emotional baggage. Please feel free to revisit the earlier chapter on forgiving and loving others, if necessary. But once you have done that you will still need to set your gates and boundaries in place. For this, I pray God gives you the courage and wisdom to take the necessary steps. The last thing we want is for you to barricade yourself back in your castle. Trust me, no one is worth it.

Journaling Moment

After reading about boundaries, are there any relationships where you feel this was/is lacking? If so, what changes can you now make?

Chapter Ten
Build healthy relationships

truly believe that God is a God of relationships. We see this demonstrated in the way He relates to the rest of the Godhead (i.e. Jesus and the Holy Spirit) and how He relates to us as individuals. It is evident through the Bible that God desires a relationship with His people and the times that grieve Him the most are when we choose to turn our back on Him, go off alone, and do our own thing.

Hiding away has all sorts of repercussions. We hurt those people who love us the most when we turn our backs on them and go into hiding. You need to realise that it is not just you that is affected but those who genuinely care for you and want God's best for you. And, if you look beyond that circle, you are depriving those to whom God has planned for you to reach out.

From the creation of the first man (Adam) in the Garden of Eden, we see God set a precedent for us of how we ought to live our lives. He said in *Genesis 2:18* (*MSG*) that:

'It's not good for the Man to be alone; I'll make him a helper, a companion.'

God recognised that it made sense for Adam to have others around him in the garden. After all, He had said 'Let us make man in our image,' (*Genesis 1:26, NKJ*) and as God Himself had others around Him (Jesus and the Holy Spirit) He gave him a companion.

This model still holds true: I do not believe that Gods best is for us to live in isolation. (And do remember that we can be surrounded by people, or be married, and still feel alone.) When we deviate from the model, and do not choose to integrate, we fail to experience the fullness of God's provision as well as an abundant life. Earlier on, we discussed the impact hiding has on us – emotionally, physically, and spiritually. We can add to that: it limits our innate capacity to do the very thing we were created to do and fulfil God's plan on earth.

Throughout the Bible, I see God placing value on relationships. And when we form healthy relationships, no one needs to experience isolation. I have come to really appreciate the blessing it is to have people in your life. I have always enjoyed my own company and like spending time doing something by myself, but now I realise that for years I had been short-changing myself. Getting the balance right so that you take your precious time alone after spending time with family, travelling with friends, or spending Christmas with others is all-important.

Words cannot express the manifold ways interaction with people helps us to feel good inside. It reaffirms my hope in the human race and as my heart and soul open up to the feeling, the 'wicked dragons' become barely noticeable. It is not that they do not exist, but they do not assume the same power because I know that with God's help – and my gates in place – I will be fine.

Just remember, this whole world thrives and revolves around relationships of every kind. And when we ostracise ourselves (consciously or not), we never get to experience life's full richness. If you are thinking that you have made it so far without people, and have not missed out on much, you do need to think again. Nothing can replace a shoulder to cry on, wise counsel from a mentor, the creativity of an idea when two or more brains connect, a referral or recommendation that opens doors of opportunities, having people help you accomplish your assignment, or even having one or more people praying for you – not to mention a hug and a smile. Nothing can take the place of the grace, love, compassion and support we get from those who God sends our way – as His representatives on earth to demonstrate His love. Nothing!

God has made provision for you to live your best life. The table has been prepared. You just need to embrace what has been made available to you – regardless of your life experiences. If you have experienced hurt and pain caused by others, please remember: there is life beyond that experience. I am hoping this book is helping you realise just that.

Journaling Moment

Take a moment to consider and evaluate the relationships you have. Is there work to be done in this area?

You won't get on with everyone!

Let's get one thing straight: you will not get on with everyone. So there is absolutely no point trying your darn hardest. It will not work. Plus you will find yourself simply making a switch from hiding to becoming a people-pleaser. The wonderful thing about people is we are all different, with different personalities and quirks. And all this is Gods intention:

If you were to look at the *Amplified Bible* version of *Genesis 2:18,* you would find this:

'Now the Lord God said, It is not good
(sufficient, satisfactory) that the man should be alone;
I will make him a helper meet (suitable, adapted,
complementary) for him."

Notice that it refers to providing 'suitable', 'adapted' and 'complementary' companions. We tend to use these words in the context of marriage but they are applicable in any human relationship. And do not think that the people that God brings our way will be a carbon cut-out of us. That could never happen because there is only one you. Nor would it mean that we would never clash with people around us, no matter how similar we may be. Instead, think of it this way: when we start forging relationships, whether they be with business partners, close friends, acquaintances, husbands, or mentors, those key words need to be in operation – 'suitable', 'adapted', and 'complementary'. That way our particular needs will be met. A person may turn out to be your opposite but they may be well-suited to what you want to achieve, where you are right now, or where you are heading. Maybe they, like you, can modify their behaviour or ideas and adjust to the situation presented. That way, they might balance you out. Being able to adapt is an attribute we all need.

Of course, we *will* still rub each other up the wrong way. And to get over that, we should endeavour to accept our similarities and differences.

Embracing those who are different from you

You can probably tell, the moment you meet someone, if they are going to grate on you. Imagine, for instance, that you are a retiring, reticent individual. On a ten hour flight you find yourself seated next to someone who speaks 100 words per minute at 100 decibels ... non-stop. Towards the end of the flight you think, 'Thank God that's over. I don't have to see them again.' But then, at the end of the flight, the person suggests you exchange business cards so you can stay in touch. Your mind is bleating, 'I don't think so!' but you find yourself handing over your card reluctantly.

On the face of it, you cannot see how you could possibly get on with this person. You seem entirely different to each other. However, the old adage about judging a book by its cover does hold some truth. So, before you toss a potential relationship in the garbage, you might want to consider whether you can look past the incessant noisy chatter and see the unique person behind all of that. It is not compulsory to strike a lifelong, close friendship with them but there is no harm in adding them to your wider circle of associates. You may find, in due course, that you share similar interests, challenges, opportunities, or goals. This person could end up being just what you need for this season.

God knew what He was doing when He personally moulded each of us and tossed us onto planet earth. As did Jesus when He picked a bunch of untrained, doubting disciples and shaped them into something great (all bar one). Why not see your mission too as one that positively influences others, without trying to change them. It is about your looking beyond what you can see in a person, or what they might project to you. After all, we all know that the person we project to the world can be very different to our real selves.

Perhaps that garrulous person on the plane was a trapped individual too – hiding behind a mask.

Not everyone will be your friend

I was chatting to a friend one day about friendship and she shared an insight. Her theory was that a person who you might consider to be a close friend may think of you in a different way. If they do not reciprocate your friendship to the same degree, seeing you as an acquaintance rather than a friend, it can be frustrating or even hurtful when you find yourself rebuffed. If we were to attune ourselves to this potential issue we would not find ourselves getting wounded to the same degree. Otherwise the hurt can lead to hiding. So, if someone is not responding the way you think they ought to, it might well be that they have too much going on in their lives just now but it could also indicate that they do not consider you to be a friend in the same way as you see them.

My friend's wise solution for such situations, whether it applies to potential friendships or people already in your circle, is to pray. Your prayer is for God to connect you divinely with people who can help you grow on many levels and vice versa. And even when they come along, your prayer never stops as the Devil may want to destroy something positive that God wants to accomplish through you both.

Forging healthy relationships

Depending on your circumstances and how you feel God wants you to progress, He may be prompting you to restore previous or current relationships with family, friends, colleagues, congregation members, etc. He may also be encouraging you to reach out and build new relationships. And, as building relationships is a lifelong process, I thought it would be wise to offer you some simple strategies to get you going:

Build a community around you, but start small

Do not aim to build many relationships overnight. That would be overkill! Plus they don't happen that way. Your aim is to start small – possibly with just one person – and gradually get your toes wet. Your goal should also be to build a community of people around you. You can start by simply adopting the habit of greeting those people you happen to pass by each day, stopping to chat to a neighbour, complimenting someone on their outfit or achievement, and sending cards. This will have an effect over time. Remember, you have been hiding for a while and it may take some time for you to feel comfortable with reaching out to others.

Make friends

Making friends can take a while as friendships are built on trust. Building trust is not what I would classify as a 'rush job', so take your time, get to know people, and enjoy their company. Do not feel you have to prove you are over hiding by clinging on to people you meet in this new era of your life. People can pick up on this and may end up running in the opposite direction. The trick is to be friendly and the rest will happen over time. You do need to be proactive or nothing may happen – so have coffee with someone, enjoy a common interest, and honour someone's invite to an event or party.

Categorise your relationships

Individuals you meet or who are in your life will fall into all kinds of categories, such as:

- A trusted friend

- Part of your business/professional network

- An acquaintance

- A mentor/coach/leader figure

- A significant other (husband, fiancé, boyfriend)

- A confidante

- A relative

When you wrongly categorise your relationships, the lines can become blurry and might lead to problems or conflict in the future – all of which could send you back into hiding. So make a mental note of where the person fits in and this, in turn will then determine how you relate with them. For example, I do not treat an acquaintance in my business network the way I do a trusted friend. The latter has access to my heart, in all its highs and lows, and my intimate feelings and concerns. They see and know the *real* me. It would be inappropriate, and possibly detrimental, to reveal this side of me to someone in my business network if they have not crossed the threshold into close friendship. Then too, someone in the role of an adviser, although close, may support me in my working life but not have that place in my personal life. And the list goes on.

But remember, depending on what is going on in your life, people can move from one category to another. Your business associate may end up being a close friend, or even your significant other.

Learn to listen

When I am building new relationships, in addition to having my spiritual antennae in the 'on' position (tuning in to God for guidance on the relationship), I take the time to *really* listen to the other person, regardless of the type of relationship. This helps me gain a better understanding of them as a person. You can learn a lot about people by simply listening. You will find it a useful tool if you are the shy type or feel you do not have much to say. Simply ask questions and hear what is said in response. And when you feel comfortable, dive right into the conversation.

Be careful of what you divulge, and when you do it

Another tip is about not feeling the need to reveal the contents of your heart or tell the other person your life story too early in the relationship. Generally, I do not advise it. I suggest your focus should be on building the relationship first. In the same way that you would not open the doors of your house to a complete stranger, showing them to your safe and revealing your precious jewellery, it is unwise to divulge all when you meet new people or begin forging deeper relationships with people you already know. Let the relationship evolve. It is as if you are choosing to use the security chain on your door while you find out more about the stranger who has just knocked. In relationships you will need such a safeguard so that you do not fall into the 'trusting-too-quickly' trap.

Send out feelers first

When in a new relationship, depending on its category and how I perceive the person's role in my life, I like to send out 'feelers' by asking for their thoughts on a subject to gauge their opinions, attitudes and beliefs. It helps me know where they are as a person. Also it helps me gauge what I can share with them and the direction the relationship may take. For example, you might be out on a date with a guy and you are not sure where he stands in relation to God and his faith, though he proclaims to be a Christian. In this case, you can ask questions about his thoughts about God and Christian life. If you have decided that you only want to be in long-term relationships with practising Christian guys, his response will help you clarify where he stands. Never assume anything! And whilst he may not be dating material, he might turn out to be a good friend to hang out with, or someone with shared interests.

I have used this strategy when dealing with matters of the heart. I bring up a topic close to something I am going through to hear a person's opinion on the matter. From that conversation, I will have a better idea of whether they could handle something I am considering sharing. I recognise that we are all at different places. Whenever I feel the need to open up to someone, I now know that it must be the right person – someone mature enough to speak the truth to me with love, grace and compassion.

Not everyone has this gift – and that is a truth I learned the hard way. We do not always get it right the first time or even the second time. But as long as you have this at the back of your mind, you will be fine.

Be open to what God may want to achieve for you and through you. You might find that He connects you divinely with someone who you do not feel will fit the bill, but then you find that the person surprises you in more ways than one. Often the best connections come about because they are mutually beneficial.

Journaling Moment

Looking back at your relationships (past and present), what lessons can be learnt?

Chapter Eleven

Quit hiding – for good!

Choose to stay out of the castle

OK, you are coming to the end of this book. You have come face to face with the hurts that sent you hiding, you have taken steps to overcome them, and are now re-emerging from your castle wanting to build healthy relationships with people. This is, in itself, no mean feat – so well done for all you have accomplished so far.

Over the next weeks and months, you will want to keep an eye on yourself, to make sure those old gremlins do not show up again and send you racing back your castle. Reflect on your progress periodically and always maintain a healthy awareness of what is going on in your world, and in your heart. This can be as simple as having a mini-retreat where you can reflect prayerfully on where you are today in relation to where you were when you were in hiding mode. Have you made progress or relapsed in some areas? Are there specific thought patterns or behaviours you need to modify?

Only you can answer that question fully, although close family members, friends or colleagues who see you regularly can also provide some useful and honest feedback. You may want to make yourself accountable to them, so that they can support you when you or they might feel you are retreating to your castle. They can pray for you and stand with you each step of the way. Cultivate the habit of bringing your relationship issues and concerns to God, as well as to other supportive people. God is very much concerned about this area of your life. Do not forget to ask for His support and direction as you journey through life.

And remember: withdrawing from others for the purpose of healing and growth, in the context of a retreat setting, is fine. Hiding away in your castle is not!

Deal with 'people' issues as they arise

The real secret to avoiding your former hiding lifestyle is to deal with hurtful situations as they arise. And they will come! Whatever you do, do not let the seeds take root in your heart and fester as wounds. Just remember, that was the old you. God has brought you on this splendid journey to enjoy human relationships again. So tackle the issues head-on and in a timely manner.

I recognise that hurtful situations and other life challenges often come at unexpected times. We may not be in a position to handle them there and then. So, there will be times when you may need to put the problem and the hurt to one side, albeit briefly, so that you can concentrate on the job in hand. Distractions can be put in your way, with the very purpose of hindering you from fulfilling your God-given assignment.

I remember getting some upsetting news the night before speaking at a major conference. Whilst I could not take any time out for a retreat (even a 'mini-mini' one) as I needed to prepare my notes for the following day, my response was to pray, using these words:

'Father, just hold me together, let me do what I know I have been called to do. Let this news not affect my delivery. In fact, take it out of my mind so I can focus on the job in hand. Let it not hinder the audience members from receiving their breakthrough.'

It occurred to me that the 'news' was a distraction that could affect the audience experiencing their life-changing moment. I knew the conference was a God-ordained session and so I decided to put 'me' on hold till afterwards. I dealt with the thorny situation later, and it did require a dose of 'me' time to do so. The good thing that came out of the whole thing, however, was the realisation that God had graciously given me the grace to forge on in spite of my troubles. I was able to soar high, but on His wings! Without His support I am sure the session would not have gone as well: the 'actress/mask-wearing' me would have showed up and performed – but my heart might not have been engaged in the process. And I am smart enough to know that God needs all of me (spirit, soul and body) to accomplish His will.

Please note that the experience I described here was not a cop-out or license to remain wounded. It was simply a strategy to get me through a crucial moment.

What I do not want for you is your Princess Leanne tendencies reappearing, even though on the surface you seem to be functioning fully. If you trust in God you can rely on Him to bring stuff you might be wanting to bury to your attention with the aim of getting you to deal with it. I invited Him into my heart and, to be honest, I value the additional pair of eyes – seeing things I cannot see at times. Just remember that you do not have to carry the burden alone. You have God by your side and others around you to help.

Whenever you are faced with a painful situation, rather than opt for the easy (but never effective) option of running back into your castle, go through this book again. Tell God exactly what you feel and enlist His help. Get your accountability team involved – those people you feel you can rely on to support you when you are faced with a challenge – and ask them to stand with you in prayer as you make your way through this situation. These are trusted individuals to whom you can and should open up. We all need them. They are just one of the many resources and sources of help God has made available to us. (Others include the Holy Spirit, godly counsellors, books, music, art and nature.) So go on, explore this excellent option.

Inspiring Biblical Quote

'... I'll never let you down, never walk off and leave you ...'

(Hebrews 13:5, MSG)

Closing thoughts

Before I end this book, I would like to leave you with two thoughts …

Remember who you are

I remember going to see *The Lion King* some years back. In the story, the lion Simba's father, King Mufasa, had died and his son was made to believe it was his own fault. Out of guilt, he fled Pride Land and spent many years away from home. As a result, his evil uncle Scar ruled the kingdom in his place. Then one day, the ghost of his father appeared to Simba and gave him a well-needed pep talk. After reminding Simba of his duty, and the need to take his rightful place as the true king of Pride Land, King Mufasa told Simba: 'Remember who you are.'

Those words stayed with me. And when I lose sight of who God has created me to be (when I am in hiding like Simba) and fail to take my place on the thrones of life, I hear Father whisper to me: 'Gladys, Remember who you are.'

Hurtful life situations have a knack of diminishing who we believe we are. When this happens, we lose sight of our true value and fail to occupy positions that are rightly ours. That is why King Solomon, in the Bible, thought it was really weird seeing servants ride on horses while princes walked on the ground like servants (*Ecclesiastes 10:7*). I think many of us are not living in our rightful positions. However, I thank God for telling us, using all kinds of messages like the words in a musical, to awaken the princess in me and you.

And remember: just because people have treated you badly, it does not make you a bad person. They treated you like trash? That does not mean you are trash. OK, so they did not appreciate the gems in your mine? That does not make you any less valuable or your jewels any less shiny. God created you in His image and if people hurt you, unable to see it or choosing to overlook it, they will have to answer to the Righteous and Just One who formed and fashioned you. As for you, just walk away from them and find others who can love, appreciate and celebrate you. And if you become entangled in the web of hurt, muster the strength of God within you – as well as the help of others – to untangle yourself and set yourself free.

And always remember the words of Simba's father: 'Remember who you are!' You are precious and you deserve the life that befits the princess of God you are. So do not opt to live below those standards you are entitled to. Your royal subjects await you. God has placed people in your world, for such a time as this, that need the gems with which He has entrusted you.

You have a job to do, which you cannot perform effectively whilst hiding. Can you see those people? Can you hear them? They are already knocking at the doors of your heart waiting for you to open them. Will you allow people access once more?

Consider the bigger picture

There is a whole world out there, and many others hurting like you. But have you considered that when you make yourself unreachable, someone somewhere does not get to experience God's love through you?

Life is not just about you. God has a bigger plan. He has a whole cyclical thing going on: by allowing ourselves to be touched, comforted, healed and restored by God, we can, in turn, help Him do the same for others. I mentioned earlier that God positioned others in my world strategically, people who loved me unconditionally, to the point that I resumed my faith in the human race.

With that thought in mind, 2 *Corinthians 1:3–4(AMP)*, which I have mentioned earlier, comes alive:

> *³Blessed be the God and Father of our Lord Jesus*
> *Christ, the Father of sympathy (pity and mercy)*
> *and the God [who is the Source] of every comfort*
> *(consolation and encouragement), ⁴who comforts*
> *(consoles and encourages) us in every trouble (calamity*

*and affliction), so that we may also be able to comfort
(console and encourage) those who are in any kind of
trouble or distress, with the comfort (consolation and
encouragement) with which we ourselves are comforted
(consoled and encouraged) by God.'*

It is like God has put in place a kind of 'pay-it-forward'
system which is all about sharing the comfort and
encouragement we get from Him with others. We must
first accept God's love and comfort (which can come
through Him and others). Then, through our experience
with Him, we can then do the same for others.

Today, I can say, hand on heart, that I feel privileged
to be able to extend the same comfort, restoration, and
encouragement that I have received to others. I am
astonished at what God is able to achieve in terms of
healing hearts – and now I just want everyone with a
wounded heart to experience His help. Hence the reason
for this book.

So why not allow God to comfort you today so you
can pay-it-forward too? Do not let anyone be deprived of
experiencing God's love through you. Regardless of your
journey or the hurts you have suffered, someone stands
to gain from your life story and experience. It is amazing
how we naturally find compassion for others who are
going through struggles we have faced ourselves. It is
the difference between sympathy and empathy. God can
use what seems to be the *mess* of our lives to become a
message of hope to others.

So you see, there are lots of excellent reasons in
support of your letting down the drawbridge. We have a
bigger picture – it is no longer just about you anymore,

but about your moving beyond where you are to be there for someone else too.

So be courageous and start your journey today.

*   *   *

'There has never been the slightest doubt in my mind that the God who started this great work in you would keep at it and bring it to a flourishing finish on the very day Christ Jesus appears.'
(Philippians 1:6, MSG)

I believe that God has already started His healing work in your heart. I pray that He finishes what He started and perfects all that concerns you, princess of God.

Epilogue
Princess Leanne revisited

This is how the story ends:

Realising that she had no way out of the castle, Princess Leanne cried and cried. She wanted to get out but did not know how. She sobbed so loudly that the sound travelled in little bubbles to her father the king in the faraway kingdom. When he heard it, he jumped on his horse and galloped all the way home to the castle.

When he got there, the king used his set of keys to open the drawbridge. Upon seeing him, Princess Leanne ran to him in joy. She sobbed for a long time, telling her father about her encounter with the wicked dragon and all the years she had been trapped in the castle, unable to get out.

'I could not find the keys to the drawbridge,' she said.

Then her father took her to her room and brought out

the diamond-encrusted jewellery box he gave her before he left.

He handed it to her, saying, 'Remember the gifts I gave you before I left? I said that if ever you were to find yourself in trouble or needing something, all you had to do was go to the box. In it you would find whatever you needed."

'But I did!' she said. "But I did not find anything.'

'That's because you did not search hard enough!' he replied.

'But I also forgot the secret code to open the drawbridge,' she said.

"Oh that's easy,' said the king. 'The secret code is your name – Princess Leanne! And even if you could not remember that, you knew that I was only a cry away. Remember, you only need to cry once and desire me, from your heart, to be there and I will always come running. Anyway, now I'm back, I will take care of you. You never need to feel sad, afraid or lonely anymore!'

The king helped Princess Leanne learn to go out and meet people again. As it was her birthday, he threw her a lavish ball, the like of which she had not seen in years. She had such a great time being with people again.

After that, her father ordered the wicked dragon to be captured and kept him locked away in a faraway dungeon for evermore, where he could no longer do any harm.

And so, Princess Leanne and her father lived happily ever after in their kingdom.

The End

About the author

Gladys Famoriyo is an award-winning author, inspirational speaker and professional coach with many years international experience. She is the author of books and resources including Overcoming Emotional Baggage: A Woman's Guide to Living the Abundant Life (ISBN 0-924748-73-7) that promotes emotional wellbeing, restoration and resilience, based on biblical principles. Her third book, Healing a Discouraged Heart: Getting Back On Track When Life Lets You Down (ISBN: 978-0-9562606-3-5) aims to uplift and inspire anyone who has been battered and bruised by the storms of life. It also provides the needed support for anyone experiencing a crisis of faith, a discouraged heart and troubled soul.

Gladys is the Director of Success Partners LTD, an award-winning consulting and training leader for the development and wellbeing of women. Success Partners

LTD runs the Gladys Famoriyo Academy which trains, mentors and coaches authors, speakers, leaders, business owners, entrepreneurs and coaches.

Gladys is also the Founder of Gladys Famoriyo Ministries which teaches practical principles to promote emotional restoration and spiritual growth through books, resources, conferences and the media. It also spearheads the Overcoming Emotional Baggage for Women Conferences & Initiative which is now in its third year.

Gladys speaks to audiences worldwide and is best known for her 'can-do' approach as well as her ability to inspire and challenge her audiences to action. As a published writer, Gladys has written numerous published articles for several international publications. Currently, she is a regular columnist for The Christian Post (USA) and Keep The Faith (UK) where she continues to use her writing as a medium to influence people positively, worldwide. Gladys has also appeared on many international TV and radio stations such as the BBC and Premier Christian Radio and has also been featured in international magazines.

Find out more about Gladys Famoriyo, along with her services, products and upcoming events, at www.gladysf.com.

Contact: The Office of Gladys Famoriyo

Email: info@gladysf.com

Phone: +44 (0) 870 750 1969

Website: www.gladysf.com

Follow Gladys Famoriyo

www.twitter.com/gladysfamoriyo

www.facebook.com/gladysfamoriyo

www.facebook.com/
OvercomingEmotionalBaggage

www.facebook.com/healingadiscouragedheart

www.facebook.com/gladysfamoriyoacademy

http://uk.linkedin.com/in/gladysfamoriyo

www.youtube.com/GladysFamoriyo

http://itunes.apple.com/gb/podcast/gladys-
famoriyos-boos/id491915755

www.audioboo.fm/gladysfamoriyo

Blogs

www.emotionalbaggageblog.gladysf.com

www.quithidingstartlivingblog.gladysf.com

www.discouragedheartblog.gladysf.com

www.academyblog.gladysf.com

Also available
from the author

HEALING A DISCOURAGED HEART

Getting Back On Track When Life Lets You Down

By Gladys Famoriyo

GF Books
ISBN: 978-0-9562606-3-5

You Prayed. You Hoped. You Waited...

Yet, life is not turning out the way you planned. And now you are labouring under feelings of abandonment, confusion, disappointment and broken dreams. Deep within you, a crisis of faith brews that throws up questions like, Why me? Where is God? Why is this happening to me? Does He care? When your difficult, uncertain or desperate situation persists, you find yourself becoming weary and discouraged. And the hope that once lit up your heart has all but ebbed away.

So what now?

Author, speaker and coach Gladys Famoriyo knows exactly how you feel. And in her journey to catapult herself out of the chasm of discouragement, she rediscovered some essential lessons about God, life and everything else in between. One crucial lesson was the fact that God hears ... God answers ... just not always the way we are expecting. This can be a hard pill to swallow but one that can bring about inner peace and hope at times when it feels like God has failed to show up, as expected.

And so **Healing A Discouraged Heart** offers practical insights, useful exercises, enlightening human stories and inspiring Bible quotations to offer new perspectives, real hope and an uplifted heart.

"Healing A Discouraged Heart: Getting Back On Track When Life Let's You Down is an exceptional read. Powerfully presented with real life scenarios which the reader can relate to, this insightful and inspirational book will challenge your thinking, deepen your analysis and enable you to question your emotions, behaviors and perceptions when faced with critical life events. Truly a inspired book which speaks to seasons of life, recognises human pain and offers the encouragement that one needs to restore hurting hearts and refocus the mind on God. A true remedy for the soul"

- Sharon Platt McDonald - Director, Health Ministries, Disabilities & Women British Union Conference of Seventh-day Adventists.
Author, Healing Hearts: Restoring Minds & Extending The Olive Branch: Forgiveness As Healing

To order, call +44 (0) 870 750 1969
or email orders@gladysfbooks.com.

Visit us online at
www.gladysfbooks.com

Both the paperback and ebook versions
are available at book retailers including online
retailers such as Apple iBookstore
and Amazon

Read our blog: www.discouragedheartblog.gladysf.com

OVERCOMING EMOTIONAL BAGGAGE

A Woman's Guide to Living the Abundant Life

By Gladys Famoriyo

Milestones International
Publishers
ISBN 0-924748-73-7

It's Time To Ditch The Baggage!

On our journeys in life, we experience challenges and/ or perturbing situations that may result in hurt, pain, disappointment, grief and separation, leaving many of us emotionally battered, bruised and wounded. As a result, many end up accumulating emotional baggage.

Often, our busy and cluttered lives mean we have little or no time to deal with this as there are goals, tasks and busy schedules that must be kept up with.

Hence, we tend to bury our heads in the sand, get back on our treadmills and try our best to get on with life - with our unresolved or unfinished issues in tow. To hide our issues or deal with our inner unrest, we adopt techniques such as wearing masks, comfort eating and retail therapy, though they don't serve us.

Therefore, **Overcoming Emotional Baggage** is the perfect book for women who want to live their lives baggage free. Based on biblical principles, this book will support you in uncovering your baggage and empower you to start your journey to wholeness. Filled with useful exercises and practical insights, this book is a valuable resource for individual use as well as in a small group setting.

I am amazed and delighted. Powerful and much needed information.

- Dr. Wanda A. Davis-Turner - Speaker & Author. USA

If you have faced disappointments, you will receive strength and support from reading this book. Those involved in ministering to and mentoring women will also find this a useful reference.

- Millicent Brown – Director, Women's Ministries
New Testament Church of God. UK

Powerful, analytical and definitely life-changing! More than just another self-help book. Soothes the soul, revives the spirit and restores the mind.

- Sharon Platt McDonald - Director, Health Ministries
British Union Conference of Seventh-day Adventists.
Author, Healing Hearts: Restoring Minds & Extending
The Olive Branch: Forgiveness As Healing.

To order, call +44 (0) 870 750 1969 or email
orders@gladysfbooks.com

Visit us online at www.gladysfbooks.com

Both the paperback and ebook versions are
available at book retailers including online
retailers such as Apple iBookstore
and Amazon

Read our blog: www.emotionalbaggageblog.gladysf.com

Also available from GF Books LTD

Overcoming Emotional Baggage For Women Self-Study Coaching Programme

By Gladys Famoriyo

ISBN 978-0-9562606-2-8

This comprehensive, self-paced coaching programme takes you through the essence of the book, *Overcoming Emotional Baggage: A Woman's Guide to Living the Abundant Life* (Gladys Famoriyo). Designed with you in mind, the *Overcoming Emotional Baggage for Women* programme contains powerful insights, principles, questions and activities that aim to empower you to take positive action to move you forward in your personal emotional development.

Our step-by-step, supportive programme acts as your own personal coach, guiding you through your journey to optimum emotional wellbeing. The *Overcoming Emotional Baggage for Women* programme is an excellent companion for the book, *Overcoming Emotional Baggage: A Woman's Guide to Living the Abundant Life*, and a must-have resource for women intent on living effective lives, as it helps you put what you have read into the necessary practice.

Overcoming Emotional Baggage for Small Groups

By Gladys Famoriyo

ISBN: 978-0-9562606-1-1

This comprehensive guide provides facilitators with guidelines on how to run powerful group sessions using the book, *Overcoming Emotional Baggage: A Woman's Guide To Living The Abundant Life* (Gladys Famoriyo). This handy resource tells facilitators exactly what to do AND say – meaning preparation time is kept to a minimum. The session planner also provides information, tips and tools on how to effectively run a life-changing group. Simple to use, the planner is an invaluable resource for both experienced and novice facilitators.

To order, call +44 (0) 870 750 1969 or email orders@gladysfbooks.com

Visit us online at www.gladysfbooks.com

Read our blog: www.emotionalbaggageblog.gladysf.com

eWoman Group Facilitator Toolkit: Running an Effective Group

By Gladys Famoriyo

ISBN: 978-0-9562606-0-4

This practical toolkit provides you with everything you need to know about starting and running an effective eWoman Group. The toolkit simplifies the task of starting a group and is packed full of information, techniques, strategies and tips to help you run a successful group. Comprehensive, yet simple to use, the toolkit is an invaluable resource for serious facilitators.

To order, call +44 (0) 870 750 1969 or email orders@gladysfbooks.com

Visit us online at www.gladysfbooks.com

Read our blog: www.emotionalbaggageblog.gladysf.com

Initiatives from the author – The Gladys Famoriyo Academy

Write | Speak | Lead

The **Gladys Famoriyo Academy** aims to be the number one place where female authors, speakers and leaders are developed and given expert advice through seminars, workshops, conference speaking, consultancy and coaching. As a result, female authors, speakers and leaders will have the know-how and expertise support to stand out from the crowd and become world class.

To find out more about the **Gladys Famoriyo Academy** programmes, events, services and products, log on to www.gladysf.com.

Contact: Email: info@gladysf.com
Phone: +44 (0) 870 750 1969
Website: www.gladysf.com

Follow Us
Facebook: www.facebook.com/
gladysfamoriyoacademy
Read our blog: www.academyblog.gladysf.com

Initiatives from the author – The Overcoming Emotional Baggage Women's Conference & Initiative

Healing For Your Heart & Soul

The **Overcoming Emotional Baggage Women's Conferences & Initiative** is all about offering real hope and fresh perspectives when it comes to matters of the heart and soul in the lives of women and young ladies.

We do this through our national and regional conferences and events where we teach practical, biblical-based principles and strategies to empower women and bring about a change in attitudes, beliefs and behaviours that will promote emotional restoration and wellbeing.

Our focus continues to be providing women and young ladies with relevant, practical, tangible, easy-to-use yet God-centred information, skills and resources which they can apply immediately to their lives. Our goal is to see women mature in their faith whilst embracing the '**baggage-free**', abundant life.

To find out more, log on to www.gladysf.com.

Contact:

Email: info@gladysf.com

Phone: +44 (0) 870 750 1969

Website: www.gladysf.com

Follow Us

Facebook: www.facebook.com/ OvercomingEmotionalBaggage

Blog: www.emotionalbaggageblog.gladysf.com

Podcasts: http://itunes.apple.com/gb/podcast/ gladys-famoriyos-boos/id491915755

YouTube: www.youtube.com/GladysFamoriyo

Initiatives from the author – eWoman Groups

Meet • Share • Learn

Introducing eWoman Groups – empowering, enlightening and encouraging women

eWoman Groups is all about promoting the wellbeing and development of women. It is the place where women **meet** other women, **share** experiences, and **learn** strategies to promote their own wellbeing.

Each eWoman Group, led by a facilitator, works through the *Overcoming Emotional Baggage for Women* programme based on the inspiring, coaching book, *Overcoming Emotional Baggage: A Woman's Guide to Living the Abundant Life.* In this supportive forum, women can learn powerful insights and practical tips to promote and maintain their emotional wellbeing. Through the use of peer support and insightful discussions, women will feel empowered to take positive action and move forward with their lives.

In short, eWoman Groups is all about women helping themselves in the company of other like-minded women. eWoman Groups can be used within established groups and organisations or can be set up as a stand-alone group.

To find out more about eWoman Groups, including future facilitator training programmes, or to download a free guide, log on to www.gladysf.com.

To order, call +44 (0) 870 750 1969 or email
orders@gladysfbooks.com

Visit us online at www.gladysfbooks.com

Read our blog: www.emotionalbaggageblog.gladysf.com

GF Books LTD
Changing lives through words
www.gladysfbooks.com

My Notes